"Rich's genuine love for God and peop
book. His story is an incredible exampl
by the grace of God."

Dr. David H. Ambrose, Lead Pastor, Heartland
Community Church, Medina, Ohio

"If you are a couple struggling to blend your families and have no idea how to navigate through the blending, then you need to read this book.

This is one man's account of difficulties with one of his spouses children and the path of lies, damaged reputation, mental illness, marital impact, scarring on all of the family through the trials and tribulations that have led to now: The final destination of healing, love, forgiveness and triumph of family.

Find out how this can happen with your family. Through love, faith, fortitude and surrender, you too will see that your family can make it if you have strength and a spouse who won't give up either.

'You're Not My Real Dad' will take you down Rich's amazing and sometimes frightening journey of love, doubt and renewal of faith and show you that family can and does win!"

Maureen Burton

"Richard's book is the gripping story of a blended family's long struggle to bond and unite into a healthy new family. As a child of divorce and remarriage I couldn't put this book down, identifying with many of the situations. Like life, the story can be intense at times. However, the reader will always have a sense that these are good people who will ultimately experience God's blessings as a result of their perseverance and love. I highly recommend this read!"

Thomas Fishback, PhD

"This book is a must read for every stepparent and for every person in a blended family. Rich has tapped into the emotional strain of blended families and the challenges they face as well as the subsequent joy and healing that comes from depending on God for wisdom and clarity and above all, patience. Rich's willingness to be honest and vulnerable in this book is a testimony to his walk with God and illustrates for us a template to reach deep, stay focused and never give up in the battle for healthier, happier relationships. This book is part heart, part head but all spirit. Rich understands that being a great stepfather isn't about being 'father of the year' but rather focusing on being 'father of the day'. This book serves to inspire all of us to strive to be better parents, better Christians and better human beings while learning the greatest lesson of all: grace."

Rachel Whitehawk, CPC, CRC, Founder, Whitehawk Ranch
and the Whitehawk Institute of Cognitive Resilien

"You're Not My Real Dad!"

Encouraging Parents and Stepparents to Never Give Up

RICH REEDER

WESTBOW
PRESS®
A DIVISION OF THOMAS NELSON
& ZONDERVAN

This book is a work of non-fiction. Unless otherwise noted, the author and the publisher make no explicit guarantees as to the accuracy of the information contained in this book and in some cases, names of people and places have been altered to protect their privacy.

WestBow Press books may be ordered through booksellers or by contacting:

WestBow Press
A Division of Thomas Nelson & Zondervan
1663 Liberty Drive
Bloomington, IN 47403
www.westbowpress.com
1 (866) 928-1240

Because of the dynamic nature of the Internet, any web addresses or links contained in this book may have changed since publication and may no longer be valid. The views expressed in this work are solely those of the author and do not necessarily reflect the views of the publisher, and the publisher hereby disclaims any responsibility for them.

Any people depicted in stock imagery provided by Getty Images are models, and such images are being used for illustrative purposes only. Certain stock imagery © Getty Images.

Unless otherwise indicated, all Scripture quotations are taken from the Holy Bible, New Living Translation, copyright © 1996, 2004, 2015 by Tyndale House Foundation. Used by permission of Tyndale House Publishers, Inc., Carol Stream, Illinois 60188. All rights reserved.

Scripture quotations taken from the New American Standard Bible® (NASB), Copyright © 1960, 1962, 1963, 1968, 1971, 1972, 1973, 1975, 1977, 1995 by The Lockman Foundation Used by permission. www.Lockman.org

ISBN: 978-1-9736-7316-3 (sc)
ISBN: 978-1-9736-7318-7 (hc)
ISBN: 978-1-9736-7317-0 (e)

Library of Congress Control Number: 2019912717

Print information available on the last page.

WestBow Press rev. date: 06/11/2020

THANK YOU......

Thank you to our Lord Jesus Christ who never gave up on us and who kept us going when we were out of strength and even when it seemed like going on was a waste of life.

Thank you to my wife and kids who all never gave up and to our families who were also drawn into the drama and mess but forgave often and never stopped loving. A special thank you to Connie and Lizzie who read the book several times during the process and offered their thoughts.

Thank you to Pastor Dave, Maureen, Tom, and Rachel who took time out of their lives to read this book and offered their honest comments and critiques. Thank you for your wonderful recommendations of this book to others.

Last, thank you to our great friend Julie who got me to believe I could do this and who lovingly never stopped nagging me to get it done.

CONTENTS

MORE ABOUT THE AUTHOR

Trouble-maker, greaser, hippie, bodybuilder, carpenter, businessman, husband, pastor, friend, mentor... these are all words that have described Richard Reeder at one time or another (or so I've heard), but the word that best describes him, if you ask me, is "Dad."

He taught me how to tie my shoes and how to draw. He helped me build school projects and inventions. When we joined Indian Princesses, his name became "Mountain Thunder." (Mine was "Sparkling Water.") He has always gone out of his way to make me feel loved, and I'll never forget the special Valentine's gifts he left on the bathroom counter for me each year.

He's the guy that showed me what it looks like to love God. I fondly remember waking up on any given day and coming out to the great room or the kitchen and seeing him there with his Bible and a few other books and a pen, knowing he had been there a while. He was determined to know God and to be the best version of himself that he could be and in so doing taught me to desire the very same.

My dad is and always was a man of integrity. He always strived to do the right thing, many times even to his own disadvantage. If doing the right thing meant he didn't fit in with the crowd, that was okay by him. He is also one of the most thorough people I know. To this day, I have never seen him do anything without giving it 110%, including the job of being both a dad and a "stepdad." He gave it everything he had, and at times, it truly brought him to his knees. Him and Mom both. And for that I am grateful.

I believe that the trials we face allow God to transform us into the image of His Son. They call us to depend on our Heavenly Father in a way we would otherwise have never known. And this dependence is something that we pass down from generation to generation. So, ya, it probably felt like a big mess for a long time, and I'm sure Mom and Dad both wanted to quit. But they endured, through the strength and power of Jesus, and we made it through.

And now, by the grace of God, we are finally becoming the family we had each always longed for. A family who loves God, loves each other, and is teaching the next generation to do the same. To God be the glory!

by Lizzie, our youngest daughter

CHAPTER 1

Why?

Why am I putting years of some of the most difficult times of my life on the written page? That is a very good question, and one I have asked myself several times.

My life as a stepdad covers many years. Over those years, I wondered time and time again why we as a family had to endure such awful times. I wondered what I had done wrong to deserve this? Was all this some type of punishment for my reckless younger years? Had I angered God?

As with all of us, such thoughts of "why" pop into our minds when things go wrong. I found comfort for the occasional non repetitive life events in various Scriptures. I learned that enduring hardship would make me compassionate toward others who were also living in hard times. That small tidbit of understanding took some of the pain of hardship away. It helped me understand my suffering in those smaller, occasional times now had a purpose and value and helped me to not feel as frustrated. However, those comforting ideas could not be applied to my experience as a stepdad. The war within our family had gone on way too long for it to fall in line with my understanding of developing compassion. These times were not simply a one-time thing. In earlier years the battles in our home were occasional but sadly grew over time to be nearly an everyday occurrence eventually fading again to occasional issues.

The decision to put it all on paper came about because of two things. First, I have shared our experiences with others who have encouraged me to share them with a larger audience. Because of their support or in our friend Julie's case, loving but ceaseless and much needed nagging, I decided to put part of our life on paper. I have also been able to realize if one person is encouraged because of our journey, value will have been given to the journey itself, along with the misery.

Second, God's encouragement to pen this came to me through Scripture. For several years I refused to accept that nothing good has or could ever come of half a lifetime of struggle. With that thought haunting me, a Scripture caught my attention and touched my heart. I will share that Scripture and encouragement later.

Day after day, year after year, I hoped the battles, struggles, and hardships might finally come to an end. Day after day, year after year, they continued. At times I was hopeful while at other times I believed this would not end well. While at times very close to it, God never let me go off the deep end. Instead, He kept giving me more patience and more strength; although, gaining it was painful. I know I never could have endured those times without Him. On my own, I may have run away or even ended my own life to escape the torment. Several times I had thoughts of both. There were times that desperation oozed from my every pore, and no matter how many times I mentally tried to wash it away, it lingered. I screamed, I yelled, I stomped my feet. I pleaded, I ranted and raved, I dreamed, I wished it would just be over.

While life is full of a variety of experiences, this book is dedicated to one thread that had woven itself consistently through those particular twenty-seven desperate years, about forty percent, of my life. I believe God has directed me to share these experiences with you. I believe it is my job to write it and leave the good it might do up to Him.

I have been married three times, and in each marriage and in life in general, I have always done my best to live with the right motives and heart. Life doesn't always cooperate, and often times things fall short of what you expect. Often, we fall short of what we expect. Sometimes life crashes or tosses you a fast ball high and outside, making you swing and miss. It is just one of those swing and misses that lasted the many years I am sharing here.

Close up, I have seen the hurt of divorce and what happens to adults and children. I have seen promises made and never kept and have witnessed what separation of a family can do to everyone, especially the kids. I have experienced coming into a family as a stepdad and seen what, in some cases, that can do to the children, the original family, the extended family and the stepparent, not to mention the impact of adding a new baby.

As a young adult, I experienced the divorce of my own mom and dad. I watched my father cry himself to sleep on my couch. I have seen the pain in my mother's eyes. I have felt the pressure, perhaps self-imposed, to choose sides. I have seen great discomfort at family gatherings and have experienced the same emotions myself.

Being a stepparent is the toughest thing I have ever done. I have had health issues over and over with no explanation of what they were. I have had financial problems, having to give up my business, home, and all the toys. I have had my character attacked unjustly and lived with a feeling of failure for many years. Many of these things were brought about by the dynamics of our blended family.

Considering such difficulties, none of them came close to what I have experienced as a stepdad. Being a stepdad is by far the most difficult and heart-wrenching thing I have ever done. For other stepdads, it is the most wonderful thing that has ever happened. Those two previous sentences express the fact there is a wide range of results and experiences in blending families. I wish I had gone into that situation wiser and with a better understanding of things that can happen when families blend. I went in thinking that all would be near perfect just like a good movie with me in the lead role played by someone like Jimmy Stewart.

I know that there are many blended families that have grown and thrived in amazing ways, I salute you, you are blessed. I write this not to those blended families, but to those families that are struggling. I hope what I share here will give you encouragement and perhaps the determination to see it through.

I write also to moms or dads who may be considering leaving their families. I have seen the dynamics of those decisions in ways I never would have had I not been a stepparent as well a child myself witnessing my parents' divorce. So many lives are affected by families giving up and separating. I know there are many valid reasons to end a marriage, some even lifesaving. I also know there are many reasons, as in my divorces, that are so weak that divorce should not have happened. I wish at those times someone would have taken me aside and helped me realized how foolish I was being.

As I have lived, I strive to grow wiser from life's experiences. I reflect on the past to see how I might do things better in the future. I look at who I am now and acknowledge how life has changed me. Having reflected on such things, I hope I will make better choices in the future.

This is the story of years of living with a difficult child. Daughter to my wife and stepdaughter to me. This child was the center of our lives but not

3

in a good way. The relationship and interaction with her dominated our time and efforts out of necessity rather than choice. From her point of view, she may say it was twenty-seven years of dealing with the worst stepfather ever.

My wife often referred to her as strong willed, which if applied to good things, would be wonderful. In our case, from my perspective, her strong will was applied to her seemingly wanting to destroy our marriage and make life as miserable as she could. Those years were riddled with leave or stay decision moments for me. I often found myself overwhelmed and not living a life even close to the one I wanted. It was in those moments, I wanted to run as fast and far as I could and never look back. Living alone for the rest of my life would be a hundred times better than living the way I was. I didn't care about the promises I had made, I didn't care who would have to pick up the pieces. I was desperate and selfishly wanted to save myself.

In this, you will see events and situations repeat themselves over and over. Sharing the repetitiveness is intentionally done, so that as you walk this path with me, you may feel the frustration and desperation I felt. At times, you may feel as I did, wondering if it would ever end. Please, hang in there and stick it out with me. I think you will be glad you did. I am, even now, dumbfounded regarding what we went through, and the things we had to do. This is not only the story of us doing what we had to do, but a story of surviving the journey.

I can't say how many of my stepdaughter's actions were deliberate and planned, or how many were just circumstance, but it was tough. At times, looking back, I wonder why I didn't run away early on. Things started slowly with the typical kid resisting doing as she was told, but by fourth grade, her behavior had changed to include some very serious actions.

My wife and I were called to school to address a "situation." There was a girl in our daughter's class who apparently had been bullying our daughter. Our daughter was typically loud and even confrontational but never seemed to be hostile. Our daughter had taken all she could take, and rather than come to us or go to her teachers, she took things into her own hands.

She snuck a knife out of the house and onto the school bus. She let that girl know she was carrying it, and that she would have no problem using it. Of course, the girl called her mother, and you can imagine what followed. This was our first real glimpse into what was yet to come.

We were an average, nice neighborhood, middle class family, yet this little fourth grader came up with this as a solution to her problem. We were shocked and caught completely off guard.

4

Unknown to me, the years ahead would be filled with counselors, police, court, emergency rooms, fighting, rage, homelessness, jail, harassment, accusations, overdosing, drugs, and alcohol. There were things I never believed I would have to experience or endure. There were things I never imagined would be part of our everyday family life. This life was as far as it could be from the Hollywood movie I imagined starring Jimmy Stewart as the stepdad.

She was on a path of destruction no matter what we or professionals attempted to do to change the course of her life. As time passed, I wondered whose destruction that path would lead to, hers or ours. She was like a tornado turning everything in her path upside down. Our hope faded in years twenty-four and twenty-five, believing this would not end well. In my heart, I truly did not believe she would live through it.

I want to make clear what this book is not about. It is not about judging, condemning, or being critical of anyone. In all of this, we have all made mistakes and could have done better. I am not trying to hurt or embarrass anyone. I am not getting even or attempting to justify my behaviors or actions because at times, I was wrong, and I readily admit it.

I am not on some foolish quest for revenge and mean no harm. Writing our story is not without some fear of retaliation from our daughter or some of the family, but I truly believe God had led us to share these experiences for a good purpose.

In fact, to this day, I ask God to forgive me for anything I have done wrong or could have done better. The thought of doing anything that would have resulted in hurting or damaging anyone else is a heavy burden.

I truly feel moved by God to share our particular situation, believing perhaps it might somehow help someone else get through something similar while keeping their family intact.

Last, all that is included here is to the best of our recollection. Much of this happened so long ago, that there could be incidents that are out of place regarding timing. However, we have gone over this several times, thinking that we have everything placed correctly.

Thank you for taking this journey with us, I pray it brings some good into your life and glorifies God in some small way.

CHAPTER 2

Beginnings

It may be helpful for you to understand how my wife and I grew up, what our dreams were like and what family was to us. It was during those years we developed an image of what family life should be through how we loved and lived as a family. I will share some of my life growing up while sharing my wife's family life a bit later.

Growing up in Ohio came with all manner of hopes and dreams. I wanted to be a race car driver, live in California, be a bodybuilder, and play the guitar. Like all young persons, I dreamt countless dreams during my journey from childhood to adulthood. Some of those dreams did come true, but intertwined in my life were also many things I never expected, dreamed of, or wanted.

I was an everyday normal kid. I fell in love for the first time in the third grade, got pounded with a purse full of rocks on the playground by a girl in the fourth grade, got my face washed in the snow by two guys every day after school in the fifth grade, gashed my leg open playing freeze tag at school and burned a field down three blocks from our house in the sixth grade. I fell in love again in the seventh grade and grew really long hair and got in trouble for using a very bad word in the eighth grade. I busted the older of my two younger sister's head open with a misdirected rock in the ninth grade and created a lifelong fear of the sugar bowl in our youngest sister by threatening to put her in it if she didn't do what I told her to do. Today, both sisters and I relive and cherish the craziness of our growing up together. We have never experienced any notable conflict, and we love each other very much.

High school came and went without any major episodes, except for me having a seizure in the hall during a class change. It was a bit embarrassing being taken away on a stretcher with half the school watching. That event was just part of my adolescent bout with Epilepsy.

You won't see my picture or name among any listing of clubs, theatrical productions, sports teams, class officers, or academic clubs, but I was there. If I remember right, my class ranking was a bit below the middle of the class which was an accurate reflection of my interest in school. School was not even close to being one of the places that held my interest. School, for me, was to be endured until I was free to embark on my life quest and make my own mark on life.

I lived in what I considered to be a great home. In my opinion, it was not far from the Cleaver family portrayed on the TV show, *Leave it to Beaver*. We went to church regularly and ate dinners at the kitchen table as a family while we shared the adventures of the day.

Dad had been a window washer, washing windows on the outside of the tallest building in Cleveland at that time. He had also been a gun carrying employee while working for a security alarm company. However, for most of my life, I only knew of Dad operating heavy construction equipment, and when I think really hard, I can still smell diesel fuel as I did when I hugged him on his arrival home from work. He was strong and always tan. I later learned my great-grandmother on my father's side was 100 percent Arapaho Native American which may explain why he was one of the few people who was tan during our nasty Ohio winters. That impression of him recently faded when my mom told me he was always white from the waist down and often sat in front of a sun light to keep his tan. The Arapaho part remained true for many years, and I was proud of it. Then there was the DNA test I took to prove it, and sadly, I have no Native American in me.

I frequently challenged Dad to arm wrestling contests, believing the day I beat him I would cross over into manhood. That day finally came, and instead of feeling like a man, I was heartbroken because I robbed Dad of something he was always proud of. If I could have a do over, I would let him win. Dad was a deacon at the church. He was a man's man, and he had friends everywhere you turned. He and I never talked much about feelings or matters of the heart, but we worked on cars, wrestled, and launched sneak attacks on each other at every opportunity. He taught me a great deal about mechanical things over the years. He gave me great pointers while I worked on fixing up my 1955 Ford. He played the guitar, which I taught him. Once he had the guitar figured out, he learned to play the harmonica, accordion, and keyboard. The amazing thing was that he couldn't read music, he played by ear. He could hear music and then, with a little work, play it. He was gifted with natural artistic talent and could draw amazing pictures. Our family encouraged him to look into becoming an artist for many, many years. One might think he never thought he was good enough, but he certainly was. He wrote poems and songs, such as "Thief in the Christmas Tree," which me and my sisters can still sing the words to some fifty years later. Instead, he chose to work in the trades his entire life. I always thought of him as a man of honor and strength. He was crazy, fun, and had a super personality. To many, he resembled Paul Newman, including a great smile and bright blue eyes.

I felt close to my dad but don't think I ever knew him on the inside. I can't remember him ever saying he loved me or things like that, but I never questioned his love. Looking back, he communicated such things by his actions rather than words. If you think about it, people often toss words around with little meaning while living them seems to be more difficult but also more powerful and sincere. I looked up to Dad and respected him.

As I write this, I wish I had noticed how some of his creativity and gifts in the arts had been passed on to me. If I had, perhaps I may have made some different choices for myself. Unfortunately, I spent my life uncomfortably trying to fit into the business world. While Dad had been a blue-collar guy, I did most of my work as a white-collar guy. That being said, it makes me smile to think that one of the jobs I enjoyed the most was when I was a carpenter building houses. I guess the apple, or should I say sawdust, does not fall far from the tree.

Now, having spent a lifetime of being a round peg trying to fit into a square hole, I realize my gifts have always been in the creative and arts world. That world is where I feel the most fulfilled and happy. In retrospect, I guess we were quite a bit alike. My mom once told me that she had prayed for her son to be like her husband, and apparently that prayer was very much answered.

If I had to put Dad into a simple sentence, he was fun and made life fun.

* * * * *

A little over twenty years ago, my youngest sister called upset. Dad had been living in her home in a spare room. She told me our Mom was visiting and Dad came in. After some small talk, he told them he didn't feel well and was going to lay down. My mom and sister chatted a while longer, and then

Mom left. Sometime later, my sister went in to check on him to see how he was feeling. She said he appeared to be sleeping but just didn't look right. I advised her to call 911, and my wife and I jumped into the car and raced to her house. The local rescue team had determined he had passed away in his sleep and were putting him into the rescue vehicle when we pulled in.

Once rescue had gone, my wife, sister, and I talked a while. It seemed we had gotten to the point we accepted what happened; although, we wish it hadn't. One other thing needed to be done. I was chosen to call our other sister. I calmly shared what happened, and she laughed at me. I can't fault her for that because I have done more than my fair share of prank playing and clowning around. I tried to help her understand gently, but I wasn't getting through. I finally had to be blunt. That was the first time I had heard my sister scream and cry. It was a time I will never forget. She was near hysterical, and I felt so sorry for her, but there was nothing any of us could do other than deal with it in our own way.

He was a smoker and had recently been released from the hospital following cancer surgery on his bladder. As I mentioned, he never said much about himself on a personal level, let alone share that he had cancer and high blood pressure. His death was caused by a severe heart attack following that surgery. He was sixty-four. Don't take this wrong, but sharing that story makes me chuckle because Dad left this world much as he lived it. He could be in the midst of a party or celebration, and out of nowhere he would just "have to leave." The man could not sit still and always had some place to be. It was a part of who he was, and it always made us laugh. So, true to form, he was living here with us one moment and then out of nowhere he just up and left. You just can't fault a guy for living a consistent lifestyle. (Smile)

Planning his funeral was a rush of activity. Thankfully, the oldest of my two younger sisters managed the entire thing. If I had done it, we might still be waiting.

I remember not feeling crushed or overwhelmed when he passed away. I believed and still do that his passing was a wonderful thing for him, all be it sad for those he left behind. Even today, I am excited for those passing on to eternity with Christ while I am sad for those left here that miss them.

The wake was amazing. The funeral home was filled with countless people I had never seen or knew. Dad had more friends than any of us could have ever imagined. People came and went while others stayed and talked. It was so busy, you would have thought some public figure had passed away. I think I met more people during those two days than I have in my entire lifetime, and it was a neat testimony to Dad. After the ceremony, as one of the casket bearers, I went to stand beside the head of his casket. The funeral director reached to close the lid, and I asked him to wait. I looked at Dad carefully, knowing it would be the last time I would see his tanned, mischievous face. I swear I saw a little smirk on his face as if he was off to another great adventure. He looked pretty much the same but more peaceful than ever. I leaned over, kissed Dad on his cool, tight forehead, told him I loved him, and said goodbye. Sadly, I wished I had kissed him on the cheek or showed more affection toward him before that moment. For the first time since he died, I shed some tears. I regained my composure as the director closed the lid. We marched out the door toward the hearse as my dad and I took one last walk together. It was one of the most special moments of my life, and one I will always treasure. He had served me well his entire life, and now I had been given the opportunity to serve him.

Now a little about my mom. Mom worked when my younger sister and I were in grade school. I remember being charged with getting us both securely in the house safe and sound every day after school. Each day we were to check and complete the chore list taped to the cupboard door by Mom. At that time, we lived in a duplex and were watched over by two nice little ladies next door. Their home always smelled of rose petals and seemed to always have the lingering smell of baked macaroni casserole which somehow crept into our house. They always had time to chat or offer us a small after-school snack should we not be able to wait until dinner.

Today I understand the chore list was not about being cheap labor as I had protested about back then, but more about keeping us busy so we would not get into trouble. Mom must have had to think hard about ways to distract me because I could find trouble anywhere.

Being pals with trouble took on many forms like playing with matches behind the couch and catching the carpet on fire, or throwing rocks through windows on the farm because I wanted to see how good a shot I was, not to mention I liked the sound of breaking glass.

Then there was the field fire incident. Let me elaborate on that little story. A friend and I went to play in a huge field that was bordered by railroad tracks. We used to walk and run those tracks on a regular basis. At times we would run alongside the train to see if we could figure out how to jump into a box car as we saw cowboys do on TV.

On this trip to the field, we carried a handful of arrows and a bow. Oh yes, along with some cloth and a pack of matches. If we had used our heads, we would have seen this was a disaster just waiting to happen. At that point in our lives, using our heads didn't seem to happen much.

We got out into the field, lit an arrow, and shot it straight up into the air. It soared through the air with a small flame trailing behind it. It made us feel like participants in a Viking movie! How cool was that? The arrow landed nearby, and we immediately put out the small fire. It strikes me that we never considered an arrow could actually land on the top of one of our heads even though one my friend shot went straight up and came straight down, missing him by only an inch or two. In fact, we laughed about it.

We did this several times with no problems at all. Then there was that one arrow. We fired it straight up, but by then the wind had kicked up, and it landed a very long distance from where we were standing. The wind also fanned the flame on the arrow once it struck the ground. We ran as fast as we could. We saw the fire grow and grow as we got closer. We got to the arrow and did everything we could to put out the fire.

It was no use, the fire was too large, and we were getting trapped by it. All we could do was run. We each ran to our own home, and I sat on my front steps. I heard fire alarms going off in the fire station a couple blocks away and I sat in fear as several trucks raced down our street. I was sure to be jailed or executed on this one! I was sick and knew I had done a very bad thing.

The next day my friend and I went back to the huge field to see it almost completely gone. Indeed, we had done a very bad thing. This was one of the few times I got away with something except for the haunting guilt I carried.

Back to Mom's after school rules; once chores were done, we had to have our homework completed before she got home. After chores and Mom's return home came dinner and dishes. Then came my much-awaited freedom to explore and run around the neighborhood far from watchful eyes. How could you have true adventures if Mom always had eyes on you? I could run as hard and far as I wanted. I could even get as sweaty as I could but I had to always be mindful on the setting sun for there would be a hefty price to be paid for not being in the house within five minutes of the front porch light being turned on. That price was usually being held hostage in the house for a few days preventing me from living the adventures I yearned for. That schedule kept us busy and out of trouble. Good thinking Mom.

As I grew older, Mom was the one I spent hours and hours with questioning life and all that it meant. And boy, did I have questions. She was the one who guided my sense of right and wrong and corrected me when I was out of control. Being an adventurous child, I saw how she dealt with me and my yearning for thrills. I knew how it felt when we were at odds and disagreed. She had the ability to talk with me during a disagreement in such a way I would not go off the deep end. I didn't know it at the time, but I was learning conflict resolution. We never yelled or screamed at one another, we talked through anything and everything. I was taught to determine what the right thing was and then do it, even if I didn't like it. Many years from then, I would use the same teachings on my children and expect the same cooperation and results. It was simple, easy, painless, and created a calm home life for all of us.

I only remember one time when Mom seemed really angry, caused of course, by me doing something I should not have done.

During the early years, my sister and I shared a room. We each had a bed and never thought we were being deprived by not having our own rooms. I instigated a game of "let's jump back and forth to each other's bed" when we were supposed to be going to sleep. Mom heard the racket and was not happy. Funny, she didn't go after my sister, she just blamed me. I guess at an early age, I was the go-to guy.

I watched her acting all angry which was so out of character for her. It was hard to believe she was really that mad. Seeing her like that made me laugh so hard on the inside. Maybe she was never really that mad but only acting mad to get the desired result. I guess I may never know.

I was in trouble, not a rare occurrence, and she was letting me know it. Try as I may, I just could not hold it back and laughed out loud. That one time I did see her real anger, I think. Even though it was a disciplining moment, it is also a cherished one that we laugh about even today.

When I was in eighth grade, we moved to the suburbs, and she became a stay-at-home mom. She spent countless hours trying to get me to study. We butted heads on studying and homework a lot. I never, ever brought my books home from school. She finally came up with a strategy that crushed my resistance. The warning was, if I didn't bring my books home from school, she would immediately put me in the car, drive me to school, and walk me down the hall to my locker while holding my hand. Game over! My books saw something they had never seen before, the world outside school.

She spent even more hours just simply talking with me about the valuable things of life. She was the guiding voice whose words often kept me from going too far over the line even to this day. She instilled value, integrity, and a caring for others in me. Much of who I am and much of what lies in my heart came from those hours at the kitchen table talking until one or two in the morning over several pots of coffee. She spent years helping me attempt to discover my own meaning of life.

Those were wonderful moments, and I hoped to have such times with my children. I hope I have been able to make my children feel like they are my life's biggest priority and guide them into adulthood with a wisdom such as my mom seemed to have.

Sometime during those years, Mom and Dad surprised us with a baby sister, turning us into a family of three kids. It was exciting to wonder who this new little person would turn out to be.

Mom had a creative side as well. She made her own artificial plastic plants. She had different color liquids and used all kinds of leaf molds. She put the wires in them and baked them and made some pretty neat arrangements. She also made wedding cakes. Yep, the great big multi-story cakes with amazing hand-crafted flowers made of icing and intricate borders and such. If she had kept that up, I have no doubt she would have had her own bakery, and I could be retired. She made cakes, pies, breads, and cookies. Then there was one particular item most beloved by friends and family alike. People from near and far would fight to get a piece of her amazing cheesecake. I would be remiss if I didn't mention her homemade cream puffs and upside-down cake which may have been tied for second place.

Every year, as Christmas drew near, she religiously baked dozens of pounds of homemade cookies of more variety than you would even see in a bakery. These tasty treats had been a tradition passed on to her from those who came before her. However, Mom took it to a whole new level. For weeks before Christmas, the house would have the added warmth of an overworked oven heating the entire first floor. It would also smell of the sweetness of the small holiday treats. The house would have decorations everywhere, so much so, if you squinted, you might imagine you were at the North Pole. One would think, with all those goodies around, it would have been unlikely I would have graduated high school at six feet tall and one hundred thirty pounds. I think some of the cookie platters weighed more than me!

We had fun too. Dad worked a lot, so Mom took us to the lake and places we could go to have fun on a slim budget. She did a great job of making the summers special. Mom and I regularly plotted sneak attacks on each other in very creative ways. I remember one time I buttered two Ritz crackers with peanut butter, snuck up behind her, and pressed one buttered Ritz cracker on each of her eyeglass lenses. In shock, she looked at me with those wide Ritz cracker-covered glasses, jumped up, and chased me out the back door and down the street. I don't think either of us has ever laughed so uncontrollably.

Mom was also very involved in church. She taught Sunday School, was with the women's ministry, taught vacation Bible school, and even today serves on staff at her church as the care minister. She instilled the core of my God-centered belief structure that has guided me all my life. What she started has grown and grown over the years and has kept me very active in ministry also.

Her efforts and love for me greatly influenced who I grew up to be. While Dad never expressed his feelings, Mom continually told me she loved me. She loved me no matter what. She loved me when I was good and when I was not so good. She taught me that, good or bad, I had a safe place in her love. I am equally sure that I didn't make it easy for her.

I grew up in a solid, loving family. We had little in the financial realm, but we were rich in love, caring for one another, and family. The three of us kids had a great respect for Mom and Dad, learned a great deal from them, and always treasured their advice.

Growing up was all about family. Among my best friends were my cousins, and whenever we wanted to go have fun, we ended up at one of our uncles' houses and always had a blast. We also spent lots of time with my moms' mother. She had been married a couple times and was now single. She owned a big forty-seven-and-a-half-acre farm where we spent a good part of our summers as kids.

Most of the fun was at the hand of my moms' youngest brother, our Uncle Bob. He was just wild. We did things kids our age most likely never did. I even think we did some things kids our age never should have done. On one such occasion, we found ourselves on the roof of a two-story chicken coop. The roof needed new roofing paper, and Uncle Bob had a perfect solution to make the repairs. He placed himself on one side of the roof peak and held me by my ankles while I was hanging headfirst down the other side, trying to nail the paper down while fighting off a band of wasps. There was flashlight tag and skiing down the hill on old skies with no poles. There were milkshake fights in his car while at the drive-in restaurant, ice skating outside at an outdoor skating rink while the snow fell, and the list goes on and on. It was the greatest place on earth for quite some time, and we loved every minute of it, and Uncle Bob had to have been the greatest uncle ever.

Sadly, our younger sister was not around for the farm adventures. Often when the three of us are together, the oldest sister and I will start talking about one of the farm stories, pause, and say to the younger sister, "Oh, sorry, that's right...you weren't around yet." Always good for a great laugh.

Christmas Eve was the biggest family get together of the year. Christmas Eve dinner was attended by all the aunts, uncles, and cousins. You had to be family to partake in the dinner, no friends were ever allowed. Following dinner, we exchanged gifts then headed off to church for the candlelight service. It took all the strength we cousins had to keep from giggling during the service in anticipation of what was yet to come.

After the service, it seemed like half the world would show up at our house. Mom and Dad always invited all their friends and families. It was a mix of incredible excitement with controlled confusion. People and food were everywhere, and Dad played the guitar for hours in the kitchen leading us all in Christmas carols. It was wall-to-wall people filled with the most Christmas spirit I had ever experienced. Yes, growing up as a Reeder was pretty good.

As I wrote earlier, Dad kept his personal life to himself, but as we later found out, so did Mom to some degree. No, they were not CIA agents, although that would have been very cool. However, there was one thing we were quite curious about. We could not figure out why they had this new Mom and Dad thing of taking drives by themselves. We would be hanging around as usual, and with no warning, they would tell us they were going for a ride. It was quite odd. It wasn't long before we found out why. They announced they were getting divorced. Can you imagine the shock? We were seeing a new episode of *Leave it to Beaver* where Mr. and Mrs. Cleaver went separate ways. We had absolutely no idea.

Mom and Dad never, ever argued or fought in front of us. In fact, arguments in our house were nearly nonexistent. I imagine their desire was to protect us from such a thing. In light of that new revelation, we understood the purpose of those Mom and Dad car rides.

We all got through it on a variety of levels, and we all have different memories and feelings, but we did remain a family. Mom stayed in the house, and Dad moved out. He was included in holidays and birthdays and seemed to always show up. Sometime prior to all this, I had gotten married and moved out. A good amount of time passed, and Mom, as well as Dad, remarried. Dad eventually remarried and divorced a third time while Mom is still married.

None of that was ever ugly for me, but it was uncomfortable and awkward at times. I never saw hate or anger. I never really blamed either of them or anyone else. My belief then and even today is that even though they are parents, they had a right to live their lives as they saw fit without consulting us. I hold no grudge nor blame them for anything in my life. They lived their lives, and I have lived mine. I can never blame them for anything I have done nor how my life has gone. Unlike so many kids today, I believe I am responsible for my own decisions and truly believe no harm came to me because of their choices.

With all these pages in mind, you may have some idea of what I believed family life should be. You can understand what my expectations of a family were. We were a close, caring, and loving family no matter what. There was no fighting, manipulating, or arguing. Even during the divorce, there were no family issues. We never blamed our parents or their divorce for any problems we might encounter later in life. We were a family, and that meant something very special to us.

I used our family as the template for what my family would one day look like. That was how I expected kids to relate to me when I became a parent. That is how I wanted to be with my kids. Maybe unconsciously, I put expectations on any family I would be part of in the future based on my experiences growing up. I never knew any other way of doing family, so to experience family in other ways would really be difficult for me understand, relate to, or perhaps accept.

As I look back, I see the good that came from them. I see the years of laughter, wrestling, love and fun. I see my every need always being met and every wound, both physical and emotional, being bandaged and healed. Mom and Dad, you did it all so very well. Thank you. I hope to be a great parent and have the same kind of family.

CHAPTER 3

First Love. Second Love.

During a class change as a senior in high school, I noticed a particular girl. From then on, I spent all my class change time at my locker staring at her through the slits in my locker door. She had long, dark hair, beautiful eyes, and everything else that made me cherish my locker time. Staring at her from a distance was about all I could gamble in an attempt to avoid humiliation. Thanks to that locker time, I finally found a reason to go to school.

One sunny summer afternoon, I was driving past the school in my white 1959 Ford. The windows were all down, and the car was filled with the fresh smells of summer. The radio played the tunes of the season, the most cherished of which for me were the Beach Boys. I looked at the school as I passed, and there was the girl I had fallen in love with at my locker. She was walking her black dog Zippy. Courage, I only needed enough courage to pull over and attempt to make some intelligent conversation. I wasn't sure I could muster the needed courage to make myself do that, but in a moment of sheer insanity, I did. "Hey there, can I give you and your friend a ride?" My hands tightly gripped the steering wheel while little droplets of sweat adorned my forehead as I waited for her answer. She said yes, and they both hopped in the car. I drove her home which I was thrilled to find out was only a couple blocks from my house. I finally had first contact with "her."

This locker love of mine blessed me with my first "real" date. What I didn't know then was that date would turn into my first real love and my first wife.

My philosophy, at that young age, was that life was to be lived while dreaming dreams. Finishing high school in 1967 put me right smack dab in the middle of one of the most interesting and challenging times in our history. I grew up with all the rules, church and life lessons that all other kids were taught. Somewhere in there I also became a bit reckless and carefree. I bought into the peace and love aspect of the 60's and still believe it was a great movement until it got distorted to include things not originally intended. Imagine a world of peace and a place where people truly loved each other. If only that could be so.

We had a huge wedding, very formal, and packed with family and friends. I have to stop and brag a bit. It was 1969, and I planned our honeymoon to Aruba. Come on now, you have got to give me credit for that one. Who, in 1969, had heard of Aruba? I was reading an article in which someone was interviewing Bob Hope. He made a little comment about his secret vacation place called Aruba. I figured if it was good enough for Mr. Hope, it was good enough for us. All we had to do was get through the reception, and the next morning we would be jetting off to Arubaaah.

What an amazing trip, I jest. Shamefully I must confess, I came down with a sever case of homesickness on the flight to New York. When I say severe, I mean I actually had to get shots of a Valium type drug at an airport clinic. Great way to instill trust and confidence in my new bride! I can only imagine what she had to be thinking.

Finally in Aruba, we enjoyed wonderful dinners and the beach. We even took off on a few sightseeing adventures via a rented motorcycle. After spending several long, relaxing days at the beach, my wife found out that the sun was not her friend and came down with a severe case of sun poisoning. The prescription given for her recovery was that she spend a couple days in the hotel room swollen, lathered in lotion, watching television. I was seeing her in a way I never had before and was banned from taking pictures - which now, I wish I had. Ha.

One year later, we bought our first home in a lovely fashionable west side suburb of Cleveland. She was moving vertically with the phone company, and I was bouncing around still not knowing what I wanted to do with my life. I think by then I had been a paper boy, shoe salesperson, bottling inspector, draftsman, and most recently, a carpenter. My lack of any idea what to do with my life put our future at the end of a skinny limb.

It was into the 70's, and we had long hair, peace signs on our clothes, listened to really cool and weird music. By the way, does anyone ever play a Sitar anymore? Does anyone know what ever happened to Ravi Shankar? Life was absolutely awesome. Our love grew, and our love for life was fulfilling.

I loved being with her but always kept a watchful and jealous eye out for anyone wanting to steal her away. I guess when you have little or no self-confidence, you live in fear of losing whatever you treasure most. It is difficult to put into words, but I think it was more that I lived in fear which showed up as jealousy. I was forever afraid I would lose this wonderful young lady who stole my heart in high school. Let me remind you, I was nearly six foot tall and graduated high school at about 130 pounds. A powerful man only to a woman with extremely poor vision.

There we were in a lovely brick bungalow, with two dogs, a cat, two motorcycles, and two cars. All that was missing from the old American dream was a couple kids.

I believe not having kids was a blessing, considering that our marriage eventually ended. On the other hand, maybe having kids would have helped us to try harder. Nevertheless, I wanted a kid. I never wanted a bunch of kids, just one, and I often imagined a little blue-eyed, blonde-haired daughter of my own. I could easily picture her in my mind's eye. Something so sweet and so easy to love. Someone who would be connected to me forever. A daughter would be wonderful beyond words.

Nine and a half years after our wedding we divorced. I was virtually back to where I had started, except now I had bills. Imagine, nearly twelve years after graduating high school I found myself to be in worse shape financially than when I was seventeen. That was not good. Everything was gone, except for my motorcycle and Corvette. I shed so many tears through all the issues, that for my own sanity, I developed the ability to shut off feelings and be done. I let my heart glaze over with a layer of stone. That process became an instinctive way for me to deal with hurt for many years to follow. If you don't have to feel, there is no pain and no struggle, and that approach worked very well for me.

My first wife and I had been divorced nearly 30 years as I wrote this, and never had any contact. Out of nowhere, I wrote her a note asking her if she had something I was searching for. I was trying to find pictures of my old motorcycle. I know what you women are thinking, that figures. Hey, so I liked my motorcycle.

That inquiry led to us meeting and spending five hours talking in the center of a little town in Ohio. I realized, after our talking, how skewed the events and timing of things had become in my mind. She thought, I thought, she said, I said, just like most divorces. That should be a lesson to anyone having marital problems. Stop and listen to the other person because you may not have it all right.

I know that my behavior, jealousy, insecurity, and low self-esteem were major contributors to this failed marriage. A marriage that at one time, had the chance of being a wonderful lifelong success. At the time, my rationale was that it was all her fault, and I was simply reacting. If I could have acknowledged and treasured the love I had for her and been honest about my feelings, things might have been different. If only I had exercised patience and wisdom, our marriage may have survived. Instead, my actions were those of a reckless, vengeful person who terribly hurt the person he loved so much. Had I stopped being a victim and become a righter of wrongs and a repairer of the now broken promises I made at our wedding, the outcome would surely have been one to celebrate.

Sometime during our meeting, it no longer mattered to me what part she may have had in the demise of our marriage. What mattered a great deal to me in those five hours was I had a clearer picture of what I had done wrong. I could not understand how I could have loved this person so much yet be more concerned for myself. I realized that love may change, but it never really goes away. I was now able to honestly and sincerely apologize, something we both needed to have happen.

Looking at our relationship through clearer eyes, I truly believe our greatest weakness was that we didn't have God in the center of our lives and marriage. We had nowhere to turn and no one to help us in the midst of those troubles. With God, we would have had a set of standards and truths to set our opinions against and know right from wrong. If having a relationship with God had been important to us, and we had at least one of the super strong Godly attributes such as love, joy, peace, patience, kindness, goodness, faithfulness, gentleness, or self-control as listed in Galatians chapter five, we may have had a chance to work it out. If so, we could be celebrating nearly 50 years of marriage. It seems when anger enters in, such attributes as love, patience, and kindness take a back seat to mistrust, blame, fault finding, disgust, and a bunch of their friends.

What I have taken from this is that when you allow pride and judgmentalism to take the place of the love and caring that brought you together, you are in deep trouble.

When we separated, we both moved to new homes, new friends, and new adventures. Separation to me was just a prerequisite to the divorce. Reaching that point for me was what caused me to shut down and accept the inevitable. With the fate of my marriage on a sure path to divorce, I set out to find new and exciting adventures. My first was as a delegate to the national convention of a sports organization meeting in San Antonio, Texas. Unknown to me, my second wife-to-be, was also in attendance. Our meeting could easily be used as a script for a romance movie. We met in a meeting, had lunch, and spent every evening walking and talking along the river among all the eateries and beautiful lights. The connection was instant, and that week was the fuel that ignited our hearts.

This new romance brought exciting flights and road trips to and from Ohio and Indiana. She was sensitive and romantic as well as an amazing athlete. She could beat me at racquetball, taught me to ski, and really brought me out of my shell. She taught me to enjoy traveling and to enjoy the little and finer things of life. She had the ability to take something so normal as eating and make it special every time. We always ate fresh food on china dishes with silver utensils, drank special home-ground coffee from beans for every cup, and sat in awe of every sunset. Now this had the potential of being what I imagined love, romance, and a relationship should look like. Things were so amazing that I successfully did everything I could to persuade her to move to Ohio.

We loved spending weekends together while we lived in different states, but now living together brought unexpected and unwanted challenges. We argued often causing her to move out of my place and into her own. That decision helped us enjoy each other again. Although, my lack of self-confidence, once again, brought with it jealousy and mistrust. Fighting continued, and I wondered if we would be able to preserve our feelings for each other.

I received a great job offer to move to California, just north of Los Angeles. Are you kidding me? Did someone say California? I was going to move to what I had always believed should have been my birthplace and get paid, too. Something inside me just knew I should have been born in the land of surf and sunshine. My relationship with Southern California was more than a wish or dream, there was an almost spiritual kinship between us. I was now only a four-day drive away from having my biggest dream come true.

I had been bodybuilding for years trying to erase the 130-pound image I had of myself once and for all. I would soon be in the heart of the bodybuilding world frequenting Gold's Gym and Venice Beach. Life was amazing, and now was just plain perfect with this incredible opportunity.

I loaded my Corvette, and off to the West Coast I went. It was a tough drive, and had it not been for my good friend Ray, another bodybuilder meeting me part way, I may have caved to being homesick again. No anxiety medication this time. Just a good friend and a beer here and there along the way kept me calm. You might be able to imagine the attention two good-sized bodybuilders got as they piled in and out of my Corvette.

We took old Route 66 across some of the country and met some awesome people along the way. If only I had the forethought to live traveling the roads of the US like the characters of the 1960's television series, Route 66, surely life would have never been the same. Years before making this journey, I watched that show every time it was on. Tod Stiles (Martin Milner) and Buz Murdock (George Maharis) drove their early model Corvette into great adventures, learning all about life. I surely would have enjoyed going by such a cool name as "Buz" or another character in the show, "Linc." Certainly, more exciting names than Richard. No offense Mom.

* * * * *

Just before moving to California, I produced the Jr. Mr. USA national level bodybuilding contest. It was also a qualifier for the Mr. America contest and had national attention. The man who won it came in all the way from Hawaii to compete. It was one of the most well-done competitions ever. It was also one very expensive show. I lost my shirt and owed a lot of money to a lot of people which limited my options regarding where to live and how to entertain myself.

I settled into my new job in the San Fernando Valley and found a cool apartment near Topanga Canyon Boulevard and Victory in Woodland Hills. Having a home began to make me feel like I had finally accomplished something. I now had to make it feel like a home. I had little cash reserve but managed to buy a fork, a knife, and a spoon along with some paper plates and a few plastic cups, some linens, a couple towels, soap, and detergent. Any leftover cash after the bills allowed me to buy a couple pounds of ground beef and a bag of salad for the week. Even with the shortage of money, this new life promised exciting adventures and new friends but also came with a lot of loneliness. It wasn't long before I was working my daytime job in the Valley and a night job at a famous gym down in Santa Monica in an effort to get those folks paid. I did everything I could to make it work but wasn't making enough progress and had to give up the apartment, of course only after a couple great parties.

My new home had me sleeping on the couch of a friend from Ohio who had already filled the other bedrooms with tenants. I was putting everything I had toward paying off the debts, leaving me zero social life. I lived on a loaf of bread and a jar of peanut butter each week. Working like crazy and sleeping on the couch every night was not how I pictured my life on the coast, and my situation was starting to get on my nerves.

No matter how difficult times were, I never regretted the move from Ohio. I only had to hang in there a little longer because I was nearly out of debt. Soon I was able to quit my second job which had been as the night manager of that gym in Santa Monica very close to the beach.

Even though we fought a fair amount, I began to miss the girlfriend I left back in Ohio. I got so lonely I drove my family back home nuts about needing to have her join me in California. Looking back, in my loneliness I should have taken more time to get used to my new situation. I was hanging onto something familiar and comfortable rather than toughing it out to learn more about who I was becoming. When I moved, we weren't on the best of terms and had pretty much gone our own ways. I begged her to move once again, even though her better judgement was telling her to stay in Ohio. She knew we weren't the best match, but with much sniveling, pleading, and groveling, I did convince her to move. She may have had some faith left in us and made the move. Not giving myself time to adjust and convincing her to move was not fair to either one of us because there was no evidence anything had changed between us. I guess there was one thing that changed, I felt sorry for myself, and she could help remedy the situation.

We found a two-bedroom condo just off the Ventura Highway in Agoura and made it our home. It didn't take her long to find a job in the San Fernando Valley just minutes from where I worked. We rode back and forth to work together every day and met for lunch. We explored and really enjoyed the West Coast lifestyle. Soon after life settled in, we were married at a Justice of the Peace at the Ventura County courthouse. A friend of mine from work and his wife were our witnesses. We had a one-night honeymoon in Santa Barbara during a hotel-filled, citywide cat convention. Within a day we were back to normal life.

Eventually, I was offered a job where she worked. We discussed my coming to her workplace and agreed if we got into relational trouble again, I would quit.

We bought a new home in Valencia only a few miles from Magic Mountain. We needed some cash to help with the purchase. The company we worked for gave us a loan for the down payment, and I ended up selling the Corvette from my first marriage that I thought was so precious. Oh well.

We now had a real home of our own in amazing Southern California. The skies were always blue and clear and the bright sun was never missing. We moved in, planted our yard putting our personal touch on our little plot of land. We bought a Hobie Cat, and sailed Castaic Lake as much as we could. We rode our bikes in the hills, and I bought another motorcycle bringing with it awesome rides through the hot, dry California air up into the desert and mountains.

Being content with setting up house as we did, we took time to train and run the Honolulu Marathon along with a couple friends from work. We traveled with our jobs overseas to places like Amsterdam and London as well as all over the U.S. We took recreational trips with the company, like white water rafting on the American River and shopping in Tijuana. We skied Canada, Lake Tahoe, Mammoth Mountain, and Big Bear. We adopted the greatest golden retriever whose name fit him perfectly. His name was Happy Dog, and he quickly became our best friend. I had gotten back into bodybuilding and had won a couple shows. We were living a dream, my dream. We were completely satisfied and believed life could not get much better. That statement proved to be right, life could not get much better, but it could get much worse.

The issues we had in the past came back. Fighting and arguing infiltrated our happy life. We argued over all kinds of things, even my bodybuilding. When we sailed, we argued about which direction the wind was coming from. When we weren't fighting, everything was amazing, absolutely amazing. Life was either heaven or far short of heaven, depending on the day. Our marriage ended after five fast years, and as agreed, I quit my job, the best job I had ever had.

The only way I could deal with the failure of another marriage was to once again shut off my feelings. With emotionless execution, I took some clothes, my pickup, my motorcycle, some bills, and left. I left all the furniture, the rest of my clothes, and all previously treasured mementos of our life together and moved out. I sought legal help and quitclaimed the deed to the house over to her. I wanted out, no matter what the cost, and when it was over, it was over and off I went. Once again, having that hard heart helped me to be efficient and ruthless in getting things done, so I could move on.

Thinking back, I see some of the same things from my first marriage being repeated in the second one. I should have learned something but apparently had not. Here I was divorced once already, and I hadn't learned anything. I was repeating the same mistakes over again. If we had just calmed down and listened more than we yelled, things might have worked out. Again, there was nothing so bad in this marriage that could not have been overcome. I think it was more attitude than problems. We attempted church but never stuck with it. As in my first marriage, God was not in the middle of our lives. I truly believe if we had had a relationship with Him, we could have made it work. Who knows, if God had been in our lives, we may have seen everything differently and never had such troubles. We didn't, and it was over. I now know, I again allowed pride to wipe out any chance for hearing and understanding her side of things. I believed she had messed it all up, and I was innocent. However, I was not innocent. I contributed plenty to our failed marriage. I still had not dealt with my old insecurities and low self-esteem issues. I also believe, with a little effort, we might have worked through our problems, but instead, we surrendered to them too easily.

Answering only to myself and having been to Hawaii a couple times, I decided that was where I wanted to live. I couldn't think of a better place than Honolulu. I was, and am, a warm weather, beach guy through and through. Once in Hawaii, I planned to become a waiter and live on a boat. The smell of the tropics never left my mind. I could feel the freedom, smell the flowers, and hear the waves calling my name. I was only an airline ticket and a five-hour flight from disappearing into my new life. Now I wonder if I was running to a new life or running away from the old one. In any event, I was taking whoever I was along and needed to figure some things out if life was really going to be different.

Without any possibility of that relationship being salvaged, I had absolutely no desire to get into another relationship. I guess I was right, I had gotten into this marriage too soon after my first marriage failed.

I had no desire to get a job in business where I had little control of my time. I wanted to just be free, lay low, and eliminate any kind of stress and crisis. I had gone from homeowner to hobo two times now. I had twice lived the American Dream of having to work my butt off to pay for a mailbox full of bills every week and was not up for that kind of life again. If my plan worked, one day, many years from now, I would be a weathered, tanned old guy with long white hair and a beard sitting on the beach watching the sun rise and set and only be known by a cool nickname of my choosing. People might pass by, notice me, and think I must know something very important that they didn't. Yes, dreams are good.

I was done with relationships as my expertise in them was obviously questionable. I was in my mid-thirties, and for the second time, I had lost almost everything except the bills. I had nothing but a couple vehicles and debt. I was convinced I was not husband material. I was content to acknowledge I would surely spend the rest of my life a bachelor.

In a way, I found it to be kind of a refreshing feeling not wanting to be in a relationship again. I could look forward to being on a boat, waiting tables, working out, running, and doing whatever I wanted. No restrictions, no getting approval, and answering only to myself. This ranting may very well be typical of any man who had no hope for a life with another person. Saying I would be free may have been less of a choice and more of a default. I had the new dream well planned out and would soon be dipping my toes in the clear, warm sea that embraced the Hawaiian Islands.

The demise of my second marriage gave me cause to realize many of us give up on relationships before we ever understand what is really wrong with them. It would be like having your car break down and throwing it away before finding out what the problem is. That is kind of stupid, costly, and unnecessary. It is ironic that when we're in the middle of a break down in our relationships, we all think we are experts. We believe we know so much more than our partner, or anyone else for that matter.

If we were all such experts, how could we let our relationship become such a mess to begin with? How could things get so bad that we could let go of a person we love? We can all be so arrogant and delusional in thinking that we are always right and full of amazing amounts of wisdom. Having gone through this twice, a more accurate description would be that we are right only some of the time, and both do wrong to our partner and are both wronged by our partner. We also can be full of self-promoting nonsense as often as we are wise. When thought of in such a way, it doesn't seem as one-sided as we might believe does it? Actually, it seems kind of even, at least in my experience. I might go so far as to add, the only area there is really imbalance is in our perspectives.

I also can say, for me, it may have been more difficult to start over with a new relationship than it would have been to try harder on the previous one. I shed many less tears this time than I did after my first marriage. Not that it didn't hurt because it did. Not that I loved less because I loved a lot. I was simply harder on the inside this time around. From now on, tears would not come easy, if at all, ever again. I found I had lost the ability to cry.

No more cares for me, no more relationships, and no more worries. My biggest concern would be if I was stocked up on tanning lotion. Hallelujah, aloha, and pass the sunscreen.

CHAPTER 4

A Wife and an Instant Family

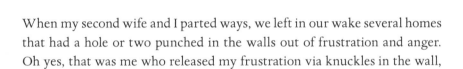

When my second wife and I parted ways, we left in our wake several homes that had a hole or two punched in the walls out of frustration and anger. Oh yes, that was me who released my frustration via knuckles in the wall, not her.

There was one time we walked all around the condo screaming and yelling at each other. We ended up standing at the foot of our bed. We screamed and yelled, and the neighbors must have thought we were going to kill each other.

This little, athletic ball of fire, born in Texas had absolutely no fear of a 215-pound bodybuilder. With fearlessness, she took action by stepping toward me, launching a quick physical attack. She stood there almost daring me to retaliate. In the seconds that passed, she didn't move or flinch, she had taken a stand. I could not let her get away with that and told her she'd be sorry if she ever did that again.

My little attempt at ending the situation did not work. She calmly looked me in the eye then launched another brief attack. She again let me know how upset she was and then got quiet. The ball was in my court. I stood there, chest to chest with her, wondering exactly what I was supposed to do.

I did the only thing I could do, I laughed. The entire scene was just too comical. Ironically, the encounter kind of made her more endearing to me. Texas women, you just gotta love 'em.

I was in another grey area because none of this fit what I had witnessed growing up. By now my vision of marriage and relationships had become twisted. I guess I was being taught that each relationship is unique to itself and cannot be put into a preconceived picture based on past experiences. I also learned that I should not expect my relationships and marriage to emulate what I saw when I was a kid. I had to learn to build my own life, not compare and copy the lives of others.

Perhaps, this time, I had actually grown up a little because this last home was the only one I left undamaged. I quietly and peacefully moved into a house with a powerlifter friend, his girlfriend, and a biker. It was just me, a new waterbed, a suitcase, my motorcycle, and truck. I was free to bring life to my dream of the tropics without having to make any compromises because of someone else.

Before I quit my job as we agreed I would, I was in my office working. A lady vendor who sold, well I can't seem to remember what she sold, had stopped to visit. I only remember she was quite attractive. I know what you ladies are thinking, that figures. Hey, so I liked attractive ladies. Anyhow, she walked in with a friend of hers who was a sales representative for a packaging materials company. It was a loosely planned, two-fronted assault on my departmental budget.

The new rep's name was Connie who was also a fantastic part-time aerobics instructor, not so great at selling corrugated boxes though. She had dark hair and green eyes. She was nicely dressed and fit as you would expect. She was pleasant, happy, and exhibited a kind of captivating joy.

We met a couple times as she offered quotes on some of our most used items. We eventually shared a meal here and there and had an easy, fun relationship. Once I quit my job, I saw her more often. I was having a great time and wanted to see her as much as I could. The more I saw her, the less I saw of my dream to move to Hawaii. I watched as thoughts of a tanned existence on that sunny island with palm trees swaying in the breeze, eventually faded into the stunning California sunset. Noooo!

Eventually, Connie invited me to her house for dinner with the added bonus of meeting her kids. The invitation was to eat, relax, and watch a movie. I needed a break from my lonely reality and loved the idea of an evening of pure relaxation. I was also ready for a good meal. I had lived a long time on ground meat and peanut butter and was ready for a change.

She lived in a beautiful home in the foothills at the north end of the San Fernando Valley. We spent the evening sitting in the backyard looking down at all the lights of the valley which were mesmerizing. You could easily see the better part of the valley, day or night, from her yard. That night, I also met both of her daughters.

The oldest girl was about eight years old. She had a smile that never relaxed. She was thin with long blonde hair and beautiful, almond-shaped, bright blue eyes. Her eye color was a color I felt at home around as my entire family has blue eyes. She was average in height and full of energy. It didn't take long to understand she was very smart and energetic. Her clothes were in perfect order, tucked in, and neat. When she wanted to talk, she would wait patiently and politely for an opening and then speak. I could almost imagine her running a company one day, becoming an attorney, or maybe running for public office. It seemed to me she was as excited as her mom to have me there. The way I was feeling that night, her potential approval meant a great deal to me, so I was at my best as well.

The younger daughter was a little past five years old. She was more of an average build, shorter than her sister, and had dark hair like her mom. Her eyes were green and full of mischievousness, excitement, and fun. If I were to guess at what was going on in her head, I would guess she thought life was an absolute blast. Her hair and clothes were a bit disheveled, as they would be for years to come. She was always more concerned with playing rather than fashion or cleanliness. Her energy level was off the charts and her imagination would rival the production team of Star Wars. When this one had a thought or an idea, there was no controlling it, it would pop out of her mouth without delay. She was a big party in a little five-year-old body. I don't know if she was happy I was there, but she appeared to think I was fun, and fun was all that mattered. I imagine she would have been just as excited if I had been a puppy.

The four of us talked as if we had been friends for years. The girls took turns sitting on my lap, asking me question after question. When we finished eating, the interrogation session ended, and the girls invited me to swim in the Jacuzzi or Cajuzzi as the youngest one called it. I had trunks in the truck, as most California boys did, and I gladly accepted their offer. It was the most peaceful and fun evening I had had in months.

After putting the girls into bed, we returned to the Jacuzzi to share a glass of wine and talk. Connie was sweet, sensitive, and fun. The girls were her life, and her highest priority was to give them the best life she could. Money was scarce which was why she worked two jobs. She had been married nine years or so and had been divorced for three years when we met. Admittedly, it was tough on her, and she often got lonely. Due to the interaction of her ex-husband with the kids, unhappy memories never left, and struggles never went away. Conflict would continue to interrupt the life of this little trio for years to come.

Her latest misfortune was that she recently ended a somewhat serious relationship after some very ugly arguments. The girls were very attached to that guy and were hurt that he wasn't around anymore. They never understood why he was gone one day and never returned. Connie never told them the real reasons until they were much older.

I was happy to be around to perhaps keep the wolves away from her door. Additionally, maybe I could help out around the house with repairs and yard work. Three pretty girls, all the lemonade I could drink, and all the popcorn I could munch, who could pass up that kind of opportunity? Oh yes, don't forget swimming in the Cajuzzi.

Getting to know Connie instilled in me a tremendous respect for single moms. I have had the good fortune to meet many other single moms over the years and have found them to be courageous, self-sacrificing, and all too often given too little credit for what they do. She was one such mom with whom I was extremely impressed.

The girls were amazing and made me feel at home every time I visited. I wondered if this little blue-eyed, blonde-haired girl could be the girl I had dreamed of so long ago. This little one, Sarah, just loved to please. She was fun, neat and orderly, and loved school. The little brunette, Megan, was fun and silly and cuddly. She lit up the room with a big smile and seemed to laugh at nearly everything. On the other hand, she was not a fan of chores, bedtime, or school and had a big rebellious streak.

I spent a great deal of time with them and was becoming attached. Week after week passed with no job and now no money. Even if my dream to go to Hawaii had still been alive, I had no funds to make it happen. The reality of the situation was that I had no funds to do much of anything.

The friend I rented the room from, gave me notice that I would need to find a new place. He and his girlfriend were finally getting married. They wanted to return the makeshift apartment building into a home again. I was thrilled for them, wished them well, and set off on a hunt for a new place to live.

My feelings for Connie and her kids grew faster than I expected. They touched my heart deeply, and I wanted to be with them all the time. I told Connie about losing the room at my friend's house and the need to find a new place. I had one offer to share an apartment with the lovely lady who brought Connie into my office that first time. It seemed that Connie was not a fan of that offer and kindly offered to rent me a room in her four-bedroom house. Although it came across as more of an order. She needed the money, and I needed a room, a perfect fit.

I thought I was falling in love, but the hurt from the recent divorce made me cautious. I was afraid but loved being with this little gang very much. My heart kept telling me maybe I could do something good here. Maybe I could help to take this broken family and make it whole again. I thought Connie could use a good guy who would be good to her and the kids. I thought the girls could use a man around to offer protection, help, and fun. I saw us as a little bunch of outcasts joining forces to one day become a great family. So, I moved into my own room.

Moving in wasn't much of a chore. I moved the motorcycle into the garage. I parked the truck in the driveway and put my suitcase, waterbed, and stuff into my new home. Because of the lack of things, I was done in a couple short trips. I had the smallest bedroom upstairs which suit me just fine. I needed a job quickly, but try as I did, couldn't find anything.

I worked around the house and took care of the yard to pull my weight. I drove the kids to school and picked them up and helped with homework. I cooked, did laundry, and cleaned as best as I could. When they were off, we would go to the LA Zoo or get ice cream at the local Haagen-Dazs, and of course, go the beach, mostly Zuma. I now knew for sure my old desire to have kids was for real, this was awesome.

With all the work I had been doing around the yard, my muscles cried for attention. I eagerly packed my gym bag with wraps and a lifting belt and headed back to the gym. I was still in pretty good shape from all the preparation for the couple bodybuilding contests I had won several months ago.

In my search for a new career, I took voice and speaking classes and met some neat people. I was invited to compete in the Hollywood Magazine Modeling Extravaganza. I had never done any runway type modeling or competing but actually won. Being a bodybuilder, I had no fear of being on stage and rather enjoyed the runway. I understand it had been filmed for HBO, but I never got to see it. Part of winning the modeling contest was that I ended up with an agent in Pasadena and a manager who was located in Hollywood. That experience created the opportunity for me to do a couple TV commercials.

I auditioned for a western movie and was selected for one of the lead roles. The casting company had photos of the gun fighters who we were to portray, and I actually looked almost exactly like the one I was selected for. One requirement was I had to learn to ride a horse. Now that was fun. Unfortunately, the movie lost its funding, and that was the end of that. That experience was great, and I did a few acting/modeling jobs here and there over the next several years to even a couple more just recently. I had a dream and according to my friends and family, acting was a perfect fit. My mom once told me I could do anything extremely well ... for a while. Acting would have surely given me the opportunity to be someone different all the time, and that does sound like a fit.

Still unemployed, the owner of the gym where I was training took me aside and told me about his friend who owned an exercise equipment manufacturing company. He was looking for a new plant manager. My friend told him about my background and set up a meeting for me. I was hired immediately. I was thrilled to finally have an opportunity to start earning my keep and paying off some bills. I had no experience managing manufacturing but did have a great deal of management experience as well as years and years of using the equipment. For the first time, I was working in a field that I loved.

I oversaw two shifts of fabricators on a Monday to Friday schedule. Both shifts were mostly made up of guys whose families originated in Mexico. These were the happiest, most fun-loving guys I've ever worked with. The radio was cranked up and rocked every day, all day. The welders sparked and the grinders ground in a harmonic symphony matching whatever was on the radio. The loud music, the smell of welding metal, and the flashing glow of the welder created a kind of music, light, and smoke show every day. It was like being at a concert. Sometimes these guys could even manage to dance when they were putting machines together. Work was not so much work with that group, and payday was always welcomed.

The new job helped, but we were still struggling. I eventually sold my motorcycle, my gun, and my 12-string guitar to help out. With the ups and downs in my life, I learned to never get attached to things because I usually was not able to hang on to them very long. I watched most of my accumulated treasures from the nine and a half years of my first marriage vanish. Following the same pattern, I also said goodbye to most of my prized possessions from my second marriage. However, I did manage to trade in my old pickup truck, that the girls hated, and got a gold Trans Am with a big black bird on the hood. The kids liked that much better. Things continued to be difficult, and the Trans Am got repossessed. Once I caught up on the payments, it was returned.

Making bad choices, getting married, divorced, and giving away all you have becomes expensive. You not only lose years and stuff, but you have to keep rebuilding. With what I had in those two marriages and what it took to rebuild, I could have lived very comfortably for many years. It appeared my financial motto was, "buy high and sell low." That is no way to build a sound financial future. Although, when I wanted out of a relationship, those thoughts didn't seem to be important. If I had used any common sense, I would not have recklessly discarded so many things that could have been of help to this little group. I think I was overly generous when going through the last divorce in an effort to wash away as much of my guilt as possible. It may have been by giving so much a way I could look in the mirror and do my best to convince myself I was really a good guy. The lesson here is you can't buy a good self-image, and you sure can't use generosity to wash away guilt.

I began doing some exercise equipment repair jobs when I was not at work. That effort eventually turned into a little side business that kept me busy doing equipment repairs, so much so I quit the plant manager job and did repairs full time. I serviced gyms from Santa Barbara to Long Beach. I spent my days driving up and down the coast of California working in gyms, and that was pretty cool. The income it brought in was also a big help. We were getting settled, adjusting to each other, and making a run at life.

Although our resources were still limited, we managed to enjoy a meal out occasionally. Dining out experiences were not always the best as it seemed Megan enjoyed performing in restaurants. She had a captive audience and enjoyed exhibiting some, what she must have believed, was a comedic giftedness. The girl did not have a shy bone in her body. We often found ourselves finishing our meals and leaving earlier than expected. I imagine our departure was often to the silent applause of the other customers. All in all, it seemed like a normal family, sort of one like the one I grew up in. I guess that normal family I had visions of might be possible after all.

As time passed, Megan began having issues at school. We were called in several times about her being rude, loud, and not being able to get along with the other kids. We were told sometimes she was even quite mean. We had no idea why she was acting in such a way. Talks and more talks revealed nothing. She would either deny her behavior or say she didn't know why she did the things she did. Some testing revealed she had problems with her ears, and that happy-go-lucky little girl ended up having tubes put in her ears. Many attributed her behavior to not hearing well, and we all had high hopes the problem would be resolved through the surgery. On the other hand, Sarah was doing great. Unaffected by the drama, she appeared content, even happy with her life, school, and friends.

After the surgery, Megan's behavior became more rebellious, and we quickly became aware her hearing issue was not the problem. Her less-than-cooperative behavior crept into her lack of doing homework, taking care of her room, and even our cleaning days. We all had chores and worked together an hour or two on Saturdays to get the house cleaned. Periodically, I would stop my chores to check on the kids to see how their cleaning was going. Not surprisingly, Megan was nowhere to be found. She found a great little hiding place and could vanish for long periods of time. Finally, we found her hiding in a small cubby off one of the bedrooms, buried under a pile of stuffed animals. Going to great lengths to accomplish her agenda was something she never tired of. Her excuses were that she was allergic to Pledge, and Comet made her sneeze, she lost the rag or was sick. She did everything she could to not pitch in. For a short time, at least three of us had become a great team. However, Megan seemed to have other plans for the future.

It was peaceful and pleasant when the girls spent a weekend with their father. Those short visits gave Connie and me time to do whatever we wanted. Sadly, the weekend visits almost never went as easy as one would expect. Many times, the girls didn't want to go, and sometimes they wanted to come home early. It often took a lot of persuading to get them calmed down before their father got there. It had to be hard for him. I am sure he knew or at least felt what was going on.

For their father, knowing his kids didn't want to spend a weekend with him had to have been difficult emotionally. For us, it felt horrible because we felt we were forcing them to do something they really didn't want to do. Visiting and trading the kids back and forth is a big issue for the split parents. It is not just a simple decision because everyone wants to do what is best for the kids but also a personal need to spend time with them. We talked to the girls many times about how important it was for them to keep seeing their father, and that he deserved their respect and love. He would always be their father, and he was the only father they would ever have. That seemed to make increasingly more sense as they got older, and today, I am happy to say, they all have a healthy, thriving, and loving relationship.

When the kids were at their father's house, they sometimes got into conversations about the past, and I hated that. Those conversations often resulted in them coming home with uncomfortable and difficult questions, making things a bit touchy. Sometimes they came back angry or unhappy with Connie because stories would be told about why they got divorced from their father's perspective. I don't think anyone intends to create conflict, but including the kids in the details of the past is a huge mistake. The kids struggle enough with the fact their parents aren't together, let alone having discussions about why. It is a slippery slope when parents share too many details of their past with the kids. In our experience, and especially with Megan, it caused horrible arguments and very bad feelings. It was obvious it was negative feelings toward her mom that played a role in her disrespectful attitudes. Megan took sides, made judgements, and got angry. She was stubborn, and once she made up her mind, no one could convince her otherwise. The problem was that her mind was unchangeable whether she was right or wrong.

Sarah seemed to process the information well, took it in stride, and had few questions about the divorce. I think she heard her father's stories and asked her mom's viewpoint and came to her own conclusions. She seemed fine with both her mom and father and went on with life. As we would see, Megan carried the divorce with her well into adulthood. It seems that no matter how hard couples try to shield the kids, they get banged around anyhow. No matter how unaffected we might think they will be, they are affected, and it is tough on their little minds and hearts.

As our relationship grew, my fears of getting involved went away. I was willing to give another long-term relationship a chance, but I still harbored a fair amount of caution. I vowed this would be the last time. Could I ever deal with the "M" (marriage) word again? I am embarrassed to admit having been married twice, and I cannot imagine what a hit my self-esteem would take if I ever had to admit I failed at marriage three times. I hoped I had learned and grown from the past failures. A smart person would have taken some time and reflected on his past or at least talked with a counselor. Things seemed so normal, I didn't think going forward required much reflection. That is something I wish I had done for my own peace of mind.

I never had kids, and the few things I knew about kids was being stretched to the max. I also never dealt with an ex-husband before and found out how tedious that could be. This scenario was very different from what I experienced in my divorces. Once the documents were signed, both my ex-wives were completely out of my life, so I did not experience any of the push and pull of having the ex-spouse active in my life on at least a weekly basis. It got difficult at times, very difficult.

Even with all the issues, the girls and Connie were well worth the challenges. Friday nights were awesome with us spending all week looking forward to a night of relaxation and fun. I even began to enjoy all those animated kids' films, eating and throwing popcorn while all four of us were crowded on the couch along with a family of Cabbage Patch dolls. We had many swims in the Jacuzzi, had fun roller skating in Balboa Park, going to the beach at Zuma or Malibu, coloring, or just taking walks. Saturdays I would make pancakes in the shape of famous cartoon characters or animals. I was particularly good at elephants, giraffes, cats, mice, and Mickey Mouse (an easy one and a family favorite), and alligators. Those shapes were pretty easy to guess, although some could take much more imagination to identify depending on how thick the batter was. Those were times I cherished. Eventually, we even added a new member of the gang, Jake. We got him as a puppy, and he grew into a huge, tricolored, adorable collie.

I felt sorry for the girls' father who never got to share such things with them. It was sad. I don't know if fathers who have left their families ever realize what they will miss or have missed. I think if I had been a father who left his family, I would have been torn apart missing so many special moments with my kids. It seems the parent who leaves might be more focused on what their needs are and at the time don't consider what they will be missing, or maybe they just feel they will get over it.

Whenever Connie's mom and dad came to visit our place from out of state, their presence produced an excitement level that could blow the roof off the house. The kids went wild. They loved Grandma and Grandpa, and their visits were hands down the best times for them. Connie's mom and dad are just awesome people who would do anything for anyone. They give so much of their time, even spending time at the nursing home with the "old people." Connie's mom is very energetic and just has a great time as does her dad. Mom is a short little lady, dark hair, and blue eyes. Dad is well over six feet, white hair, and a good build. I must add he was quite intimidating when I first met him.

I can't describe her dad without saying this one thing. I have never heard this man talk about anyone else or have anything bad to say about anyone. In all these years, he may be the only person I can honestly say that about. A very rare trait indeed.

I believe the grandparents' visits also gave the girls a sense of family and belonging. While parents may change, grandparents never divorce you, which is a relationship the kids treasured, felt secure in, and could depend on.

The obvious excitement we saw when her parents visited caused us to think the girls' lives might be much richer if they had family close by. We wondered if Los Angeles might not be the best place for them and started thinking about moving east. We could move back to my hometown in the Cleveland area or to a suburb of Chicago where Connie grew up and also had lots of family. I have earlier shared a bit about where I grew up and what life was like for me, giving you a picture of what I expected family life to be. That is the kind of family life that awaited the kids in the Cleveland area. To fill in all the blanks, I need to share a bit of Connie's growing up and family life too.

CHAPTER 5

Her Home Life

I asked Connie to share a bit about her life at home and here is what she shared.

Connie was born in the Chicago area early in the 1950s. She is one of four children, the only girl, and the second oldest. While some might think such an unequal balance of gender could be problematic, it earned her a room of her own while the boys all had to share one. You go, girl! She treasures her family and feels blessed to be part of such a large gang.

The six of them were not the only part of the family in the area. She grew up with a loving family filled with cousins, aunts and uncles, and grandparents all within minutes of her house. She often speaks of how her life was filled with lots of time spent with her grandparents who lived next door.

Mom and Dad were amazing and were not only husband and wife but had been best friends since they first met. They have been fully committed to each other their entire sixty-five years of marriage and are a rare example in today's world where marriages often seem to be more short-lived.

The joy of family peaked around the holidays, particularly Christmas. A treasured part of Christmas was the annual family Christmas card photo tradition. As the family grew older and the kids moved away and had their own families, Mom and Dad continued with the Christmas card photos. Every year all the kids would get a photo card with Mom and Dad doing something cool in it. Cards would come with a picture of them on a beach in some tropical location, skiing in Colorado, or square dancing in western outfits in the southern tip of Texas. They kept that tradition alive until Dad passed away at the age of eighty-six. Connie and I looked forward to that part of Christmas every year in eager anticipation of seeing what great adventure would be captured on that year's card.

Connie's mom always refers to Connie as the "happy go lucky child" which is easy for me to believe because in many things, she is very much that way today. Her older brother, the first born of the family, was tagged the "serious" one. She looked up to her older brother and followed him around as many places as he would let her. She always felt good around him and saw him as her protector, a responsibility he always took "seriously," of course.

Following big brother and Connie, there were two more boys added to the gang. One came two years after Connie, and the youngest was born three years after that.

Mom and Dad both worked outside the house while the kids were growing up. They eventually purchased an insurance agency and spent a great amount of time building and growing the business. Other than growing the agency into something quite successful, Dad had the chance to do something a little different than most insurance agencies. Due to a chance meeting before buying the business, Dad met and got to know the head coach and owner of a professional football team. During his years with that team, the owner had a strict policy that his players develop a backup career other than football. He felt obligated to protect the players in case they sustained a career-ending injury or other issue that would end their career.

The team's owner met with Connie's dad and asked him to mentor a young, exceptional player. That player is still around today and is extremely well-known. Dad trained him in the insurance business, and that player and Connie's family grew to enjoy a very special relationship. When he and his wife had children, Mom and Dad were asked to be the godparents of their first-born child. That player went on to become an exceptional player, Pro Football Hall of Fame member, coach, and currently a sports commentator and is a highly regarded person in sports. Mom and Dad eventually retired and sold the business, but it is still alive and operating well to this very day.

Connie was always a petite little girl with great big, full of life, green eyes, very much like Megan. I can easily imagine her being the "special" one with Mom and Dad and the boys. In her own words, she proudly proclaims, "I was pretty cute!" She basked in the joy of her place in the family and her cuteness for some time. When she turned seven, she began having a lot of earaches that were easily remedied by the simple removal of her tonsils. Even now, she can smell the ether they used to put her to sleep for the procedure.

As was common with the use of ether, she also experienced a lot of sickness and vomiting after the surgery. Connie threw up so much, they kept her in the hospital an extra day to make sure she would be okay.

The good news was, the surgery was successful, putting an end to her earaches. The bad news was, she unexpectedly and rapidly began putting on weight. Her weight gain quickly got out of control for no obvious reason. The weight issue continued until at age nine, this petite little girl had become not so petite. Mom finally took her to what at the time was called a "fat doctor." They had high hopes he would be able to tell them what was going on.

The doctor prescribed thyroid pills and pituitary shots to help her stop her uncontrollable weight gain. Some of the doctors they had seen attributed her weight gain to a mistake made during her tonsil surgery. They believed the surgeon may have accidentally nicked her pituitary gland while her tonsils were being removed. She continued the prescription of pills and shots and several increases in dosages for many years until she had an extremely bad reaction to them and had to stop all medications immediately.

In the eighth grade, Connie developed another physical problem. Out of nowhere, she found herself doubled over in unbearable abdominal pain. She was rushed to the hospital and admitted for what turned out to be a week full of tests, poking, and prodding. Their first thoughts were that she may have cancer. She was immediately scheduled for a myriad of tests in a valiant effort to quickly find the cause of the pain. Their efforts were successful finding cysts on both of her ovaries. The decision was made to do exploratory surgery to see what could be done. The surgery resulted in the complete removal of one ovary and half of the remaining one. After the surgery, they kept her in the hospital for another week before releasing her. It is difficult to imagine what Connie and her parents must have been feeling, seeing her with so many problems at such a young age let alone watching her having to endure all the pain and surgeries. During her stay in the hospital, her parents were always there, encouraging and comforting her.

The grandparents who were earlier mentioned as living next door to them were her mom's parents. Connie remembers many very special days hanging out with them. She particularly enjoyed the fact they had shiny, slippery floors. The floors gave her many opportunities to run and slide across the room in her socks. She lays claim to "inventing" the sock slide because she did it way before Tom Cruise did it in the movie *Risky Business*. Of course, her grandparents were against her doing something so potentially harmful, so she only did it when they weren't looking. She is sure had she been caught doing the sock thing, she would have gotten a good lecture about broken necks.

Grandpa was a carpenter who built homes, in fact, he built Mom and Dad's house which was the one Connie grew up in. Her mom lived there until 2016, and that little house holds many special memories for the entire family, all the grandchildren and all the great-grandchildren. When the house was built, the street was a two-lane dirt road way out in the country. It was so calm and quiet out there, no one would have ever guessed Connie's little brother would throw a wild pass and a passing car would destroy her dad's prized football autographed by the entire Chicago Bears team which won the Bears eighth NFL Championship. Nor could anyone have imagined Connie would be knocked off her bike by a car with three sailors in it a couple streets from home while her big brother watched. She was not seriously hurt, and the sailors stayed with her while her ever-protective big brother raced home to get Dad.

Today, it is a four-lane concrete road in a thriving, busy area with anything you could ever want no more than five minutes away. Needless to say, that old dirt road hardly ever had a car going down it, while today the traffic is quite heavy. Grandpa was a quiet, gentle man, and no one ever really knew what he was thinking. All the memories of times with Grandpa and Grandma are still very special to all the kids. Connie still remembers how sad she was and how difficult it was for the family when Grandpa died. He is greatly missed.

Now with Grandma living all alone, Connie and the two oldest boys took turns sleeping at Grandma's house. After dinner, they all loved to run across the stony path between her lilac bushes. At times it was hard for the young kids to sit quietly in the house, so escaping to run through the lilacs was their way of burning some energy. Connie said, "Even today when the weather gets warm, I still remember that path and can smell the lilacs."

Not only did the kids need to escape for a while, but Grandma needed a little space as well. Grandma never missed a day exercising along with Jack LaLane on his television show. It was her favorite show, but a show the kids had no interest in. Twice a day, she would turn on the program and do her calisthenics and sit ups right along with Jack.

The mornings after spending the night with Grandma, the kids would often wake to a bowl of cereal accompanied by blueberries, blackberries, or currants. After gorging themselves with such a tasty breakfast, they would get dressed and hurry off to school.

One day while visiting her sister in Canada, Grandma passed away. True to form, she did it right in the middle of a workout with Mr. LaLane for what would be her last exercise session.

As time passed, it became clear the things that had been done to eliminate Connie's physical issues had worked. One of the doctors commented it was his belief somehow the cysts may have been caused by the pills and shots she had been taking for her weight problem. All that was behind her now, and she was ready to start high school as a pain free, new, and slimmer version of her old self. The out-of-control overweight body had vanished, making the way for the new slim, trim, and girly version. It could not have happened at a better time. A new school, new friends, and a fresh start. Expectations were high, very high.

In anticipation of her first day of school, Connie convinced her mom that her new look required her brunette hair be changed to blonde. The brunette hair just would not do while the blonde hair would be just the finishing touch the new Connie needed. Surprisingly, Mom went along with her request, and Connie was shocked. She delivered the request, never thinking she would get an okay. She still believes Mom agreed because she felt sorry Connie had to deal with all the hard times and surgeries. Mom may have also felt a fresh start was certainly in order.

High school was all Connie hoped it would be, and she loved it and was experiencing many new feelings. With the exception of the younger cute years, she now actually felt pretty for the first time in her life. Fortunately, she had a little help learning the ropes of high school because her older brother was two years ahead of her and was on the football team. A brother such as him would be a huge asset for any girl. His being on the team opened new avenues and opportunities for her that were common occurrences for older girls. She was now being invited to dances, parties, movies, and Sunday afternoon roller skating.

By her junior year, she had become a member of the Pep Club, PomPom Team, and had begun to choreograph routines. She loved her new life and the support received from her parents who attended every basketball and football game Connie cheered at.

Connie's confesses her high school academic records portray her as no more than an average student. It was true because she enjoyed dating, having fun, and hanging out with her friends much more than school work. She did what she had to do to maintain a "C" average which kept her eligible for PomPoms and Pep Club. It would seem a lack of interest in school was something we had in common.

Family life was awesome because they all did so many things together. Camping was one of the favorite things for both family and friends alike. Their favorite place to camp was at Silver Lake in Michigan. Dad and the boys not only loved camping but loved fishing as well.

Mom and Dad worked hard all year, and when school was out for summer, the local pool became the greatest source of fun for the kids. It was nearly a daily occurrence to see the family vehicle pull up to the pool and drop the troops off for swim team on the way to work. Mom and Dad faithfully returned to pick them up for lunch, and weather permitting, they would be back at the pool in the afternoon to again be picked up after work. The pool was a great part of life for Connie who worked hard to get her Life Saving Badge. The staff wanted her to keep working at her life saving skills and become a lifeguard, but she seemed to always be sunburned. She may have looked like a typical lifeguard, but her fair skin had become a concern for pool management. As it turned out, their concerns were valid. Decades later, she found she had a little skin cancer like many people who spend too much time in the sun early in life. The doctors told her the years at the pool were, most likely, the cause of her skin problems.

More family excitement was caused by Dad being a Boy Scout Troop leader. He was amazing at all the Scout activities and camping which, of course, was right up his alley. He was also a member of the American Legion having served in the Armed Forces. He was the Legion's spokesperson managing the scholarships program. Each year the legion offered a financial scholarship to high school students to help with college costs. Dad met with schools and students and gave out applications. He was part of the team that decided who would be given scholarships and arranged for the funds to be awarded to the lucky students.

Another of his much-loved commitments was being in the local holiday parades as part of the American Legion. He often marched with other members, all properly dressed in uniform, but his specialty was being a clown, and what a site that was.

Mom wasn't much for "clowning" around in parades but was very devoted to doing things at the church and with the women's club. While there were times they did things separately, Mom and Dad seemed to be at their best when they were together. It also seemed they loved anything and everything as long as they could do whatever it was together. For example, a couple at church had quadruplets with health issues. The boys were named Matthew, Mark, Luke, and John. They required daily, around the clock care. Their parents could not manage that level of care, so Mom and Dad organized teams of four and a schedule to give care to the boys. They spent countless hours with the boys as one of the teams for nearly a year but never felt burdened because they shared the effort.

Mom and Dad both had a passion for dancing, and when they got out on the floor, people were amazed, not only at their skills but also at the connection they had with each other. The love they shared played out in everyday life, in everyday ways including the dance floor.

In later years, Dad made an amazing discovery. He found he loved to sing. He began singing solos at church and also at funerals and gravesides. Before long, his graveside singing earned him many opportunities to sing at burial services. Connie has also been a singer for as long as I have known her. One of her most cherished memories was singing a duet at our church on Thanksgiving with her dad.

We recently learned something about her dad during his funeral a few years ago. We learned he was a member of the Knights of Columbus. During the entire wake, the Knights posted an Honor Guard at his casket. It was made up of one Knight at his head and the other at his feet. Members of the Honor Guard took turns standing motionless and quiet in full dress through the entire wake. Full dress included feathered hats, swords, sashes, and all. Near the end of the wake, several members of the American Legion lined up in the back of the room and walked slowly to the casket. They walked one by one to his casket and honored him by each member placing a red poppy on his chest. The entire room was deeply moved, and it will be a moment etched in our memories forever.

Connie's family has always been extremely important to her. While reflecting on the stories and feelings she shared with me, she commented, "I realize how blessed I was to have parents who loved me and supported me and who loved each other so deeply."

Connie had no aspirations of being a scientist or doctor but did have a goal which was greatly supported by Mom and Dad. Her lifelong dream was to get enough education to become a flight attendant and see the world. She went to college with that very dream in mind and managed to earn straight "A's" which was something she had never come close to in high school. One day, at twenty years old, she found herself standing in front of her mirror in her United Airlines Flight Attendant uniform. The dream had come true, and she was off to see the world.

A year later, at age twenty-one, Connie married her first husband. As soon as he completed dental school, they moved to sunny California where he joined a dental practice.

In the following years as a flight attendant, Connie traveled to Australia, Hawaii, Singapore, Taiwan, South America, the Orient, Italy, Greece, and many other places. She loved nearly every place she went. Oddly, these days, I find it hard to get her motivated to do any traveling at all. If I think about it from her perspective, what is there that she hasn't already seen?

While Connie's career with United Airlines continued, her marriage struggled and became riddled with questions, concerns, and doubts. Their doubts and struggles continued for three years when they found they were to have their first child. The pregnancy went long by ten days, and she was forced to give birth. The doctors successfully brought their first little girl, Sarah, into the world at five and a half pounds. She was wonderful, beautiful, and healthy. They could not have been happier or more excited.

Connie loved being a mom, and when the day came that her six-month maternity leave from the airlines was over, she found herself hating the idea of returning to the same job she once loved so much. She worked for another year and was again granted maternity leave because she was pregnant with their second child. There was another little girl, Megan, waiting patiently to enter the world. This second bundle of joy and love was also born only seven days after her due date. She was beautiful and healthy, and Mom and Dad offered a great big, "Thank you!" toward heaven.

This time the airlines only granted her a five-month leave, and Connie knew it would expire all too fast. She loved being with the girls and could not imagine a better life than that. As expected, the five months flew by, and she again returned to flying. She forced herself over and over to board planes and jet across the country, but her will power only lasted for a month.
After nine years, Connie resigned from United and was able to live a new dream - being a stay-at-home mom. She was fortunate enough to have a second dream come true in one lifetime and was filled with more joy than words could describe. After all was said and done, trading a dream career to become a mom was not much of a trade at all, it was more of a blessing.

Life was great, for a while. Sadly, after nine and a half years of marriage, their relationship ended. The divorce was not easy and impacted everyone immensely.

All of a sudden, Connie not only found herself to be a stay-at-home mom but a single mom as well. Her new position in the family caused unexpected and trying difficulties for the little band of girls. Connie had to find a job to be able to cover the bills and expenses of the home. She had been teaching aerobic dance part-time, but financial needs dictated she get a full-time job. Fortunately, she had been asked to manage the entire aerobic dancing program at the gym which gave her the full-time job she needed. Even with that job, she still came up short and found another job selling shipping and packaging materials for a local company.

After being a single mom for several years, a friend of hers, who was also in the shipping business, offered to help her with her sales by introducing her to a few companies she already had a relationship with. Connie had no idea that by being introduced to one particular company, she would meet her future husband.

CHAPTER 6

Third Time the Charm?

Would Connie say yes or no? I was about to find out in the most unexpected way.

By the time packaging rep Connie visited me at work with her friend, she had been on her own long enough to have an idea of how she wanted life to move forward. She dated a little, and from my view, the timing for me to have a relationship with her seemed like a part of a higher plan. The length of time since her divorce made it very clear to everyone, I had no part in her marriage falling apart. I didn't want to be mistaken for the guy who broke up her marriage. With any such concern alleviated, my thoughts about making this a permanent relationship felt good.

We had become a family of sorts, and Connie believed if we were going to become a permanent family, we needed to attend church regularly. That turned out to be one of her best mandates. We became involved in several activities at church. Connie loved to sing and joined the praise and worship team. Together we did small groups and other events involving the girls.

I did a little speaking and ushering and became good friends with the Pastor. He and I had lunch at least once a week, and somehow, he got the idea that I should become a deacon. We talked several times about me taking that role at church, but there was an issue which was always in the way. The issue was that Connie and I shared a house and were not married. There was no way I could serve as a deacon while having that kind of living arrangement. I didn't know what to do and was not completely sure that marriage and I could ever work out. My success rate with marriage was not very good as my score stood at zero and two. Truthfully, I was not even sure that Connie would marry me.

Permit me to add a little fact that will make this entire subject even more interesting. You see, I had a problem with jewelry. It sparkles so brightly, and I have the ability to match the personality of a person very close to me with those sparkly little rascals. When we first started dating, I was walking through the mall wasting time and wandered into a jewelry store. I noticed a diamond ring with three rows of seven diamonds each. It was very artsy and clear, bright, and full of energy. It was just so pretty. I should have run out the door, but foolishly, I didn't. It struck me as being a perfect ring to fit Connie's personality, and according to the salesperson, opening an account would only take five minutes. It never crossed my mind that those five minutes would take me two and a half years to pay off. I also did not take time to consider how such a purchase would fit into my already, no extra money budget. So, being just like any other guy, I bought it believing I would figure the finances out later. I have a very hard time passing up shiny, sparkly things. Perhaps I was raised by raccoons or crows and didn't know it.

Many years later that shiny, sparkly problem would rear its head again but not in a jewelry store. This time I would find a nice shiny Harley which fit my personality nicely. Not exactly the same thing, I guess. (Chuckle)

The evening after I bought the ring, we celebrated Connie's birthday. I was delighted with the ring and was so excited to give it to her. After dinner, I handed her the box and waited to hear a giggle, scream, gasp, or something like "You shouldn't have." What I heard was none of those. What I heard was, "Yes, I will". I sat there puzzled and confused, trying to figure out what in the great state of California she was talking about. Then it was I who gasped. Get married? Whoa! This was not a proposal. I did not ask a question, did anyone hear a question? No, it was just a very shiny ring for a very pretty girl. Help!

Okay smart people, what would you have done at this point? I did the only thing my manhood would allow me to do, I went along with it. With no intent of getting married in the near future, I was engaged. As my adrenalin slowed down and my heart rate came closer to normal, I quickly evaluated the situation and determined I could live with being engaged. We made no plan to set a date, no plan to have an engagement party or any such thing. I simply had to remember it was only an engagement. (Note to self, stay out of jewelry stores.)

Now, you are up to date with that little fact I hadn't mentioned earlier. I updated the pastor on our status although I did not divulge the fact that I wasn't exactly planning a marriage in the near future. I tried to get him to accept engaged as good enough to qualify for being a deacon but with no success.

A few weeks later, Connie and I were eating lunch with him at one of our regular places. We ate and chatted, having a great time as usual. Then all of a sudden, he got quiet and looked calmly at Connie while retrieving his appointment book from his pocket. He spoke with sincerity and said, "So, when do you guys want to get married?" I choked on my lunch which neither the pastor nor Connie even noticed. Hey, a little help here would be nice.

Again, once the adrenalin slowed and my heart rate got back to normal, I was able to process what had happened. It seems he got tired of waiting for me to do something about getting married and took matters into his own hands. To this day, the joke between Connie and me is that I never proposed. So, into wedding planning mode we went, and six weeks later, we were married.

I loved all three girls and was excited for Connie and I to patch up this little broken family and create a good solid home. I was up for the challenge, so I thought.

The wedding was to be done by our pastor friend at our small community church. We planned a simple cake and coffee reception after the service. Still struggling with our finances and trying to recover from both our divorces (not to mention my jewelry addiction), we kept things modest. We had no way of funding a honeymoon and would celebrate by going to dinner with the girls and Connie's mom and dad. After dinner, we would go home, so the grown-ups could share a bottle of champagne, and the girls could share a bottle of sparkling grape juice. We promised each other we would one day take that honeymoon. Over thirty years later we have yet to fulfill that promise.

It was an evening wedding, so the sanctuary lights were dimmed, the candles were lit, and the church smelled of melting wax. All this making the feel of the church and this moment very special. When I walked out into the church with the pastor, I was sure I was doing the right thing, and this was meant to be. There were Connie, myself, the pastor, and Connie's daughters Sarah and Megan as the bridal party. The sanctuary was packed with the many friends who had been encouraging us all along the way. I felt like everyone we knew was behind this crazy soon-to-be family. I relaxed, everything felt right, and it all seemed to fit my picture of a family as I had experienced when I was a kid. Now it was time for the ceremony and not once did Hawaii cross my mind.

Simple, sweet, and just right. Sarah and Megan walked down the aisle, speedily as if not wanting any attention. However, they seemed to enjoy their brief moment in the spotlight while giggling but with shyness always fighting for center stage.

Connie floated down the aisle, and time seemed to be in slow motion, it was a beautiful moment. I felt lucky, very lucky, and held onto the highest of hopes that this was the family I had searched for all these years. Tonight was the start of our lives together, and a new life for each of us.

Pastor began the ceremony, and part way through, I could see Connie giving mean mom looks to Megan. She was making angry faces at her attempting to get her to stop balancing her bouquet on her shoulder. Despite all her mom's visual pleading, Megan never let up. Bored with that, Megan went on to make this feat even more difficult. She stood arms outstretched while moving back and forth as you might see one do while balancing a plate on a stick set on their chin. She happily demonstrated her skills while dramatically keeping it balanced. There were a couple flaws in her act as the bouquet slipped from her shoulder a couple times but was quickly caught with great celebration before it could hit the floor. I witnessed her cat-like reflexes making it possible for her to save the bouquet and nearly applauded myself as I imagine others in the audience may have wanted to do. Undaunted and being quite the showman, she placed them right back on her shoulder and continued on. I don't think Connie envisioned her wedding ceremony complete with entertainment. True to form, I don't think Megan much cared either, she was having a blast. Today, I wondered if her balancing act was simply a way to express her displeasure with our wedding, or if there was just another party going on in her head.

I had given a great amount of thought to us becoming a family. Here we were, that ragtag bunch, toughing out life with some difficult events pressing us up against the ropes. With all of that in mind, I wanted that night to be special and a new beginning for us all. I refocused on the ceremony rather than the little sideshow, and it was very good.

Purposely, I ignored the earlier note to self and made one more trip to the jewelry store. I bought Connie's ring and two little gold bands, one each for Sarah and Megan. I never heard of such a thing being done, but I really wanted to take a moment to share my heart. After Connie and I exchanged rings, I walked to the two girls and asked them to come near me. Kneeling down, I told them tonight was not just me marrying their mom, but in a sense, we were all being joined as a family. I told them I loved their mom and them very much and wanted to be part of their family. We had a new start and would be there for each other, forever. I gave them each a ring, they put them on, and the ceremony finished.

I recently had a conversation with Connie's mom, and she made an off-the-cuff comment about Megan never buying the gold ring thing. Hearing that, it struck me that some might think I did it to manipulate the girls. I am not sure if that was what she was thinking, but I want to be very clear, I loved the whole family and was as sincere as anyone can be. I wanted them to feel I loved them as much as their mom. I know how some kids get shoved aside in these situations, and I was promising to do my best to not let that happen.

Happy to be done and past Megan's public onstage debut, Connie and I went to the reception area for cake and coffee. While we headed back, a member of the congregation was doing video interviews with some of those in attendance. Interestingly, he interviewed Megan. I believe the question was something like "How did you like the wedding?" and her reply was "I think I am going to be sick!" I guess that should have given us some insight into her little show onstage. I can say that her comment turned out to be a prediction of what was yet to come.

We had our dinner at the nice French restaurant our friend's owned, then headed back home for champagne and sparkling juice to finish our celebration. Connie's mom and dad got the kids settled in their rooms, and we all said goodnight. Not your typical wedding night with kids and parents down the hall, but that didn't matter, it was just wonderful to be married.

We were exhausted and eagerly settled in for a good night's sleep when the loudest, fastest, and hardest pounding on our door you can imagine began. It was Megan pounding, screaming, crying, and kicking at the door.

We sat in bed shocked and in disbelief. Despite her grandparents pleading with her to stop, Megan relentlessly screamed "I want my mommy" and "Let my mommy out" at the top of her lungs. It sounds humorous now, and it makes a great "worst wedding night ever" story to share with friends over a glass of wine, but at the time, it was horrible. This sweet, fun loving little girl's behavior had put a bit of a damper on what could have been a beautiful day. Grandma and Grandpa finally got her to bed, and we all finally got some sleep.

Adjusting to our new arrangement went well except for Megan. She exhibited what we thought was her displeasure via a bad attitude about so many things every chance she got. Sarah seemed quite content, and I think was pleased with her little golden token and the new arrangement. I believe she understood what I was trying to do and allowed us to be a family. What we didn't know for quite some time was that Megan had taken her gold ring to school the Monday after our Saturday wedding and tossed it into the garbage. What more need be said?

I was hurt, and to be honest, offended. How could this be the little girl I thought loved having me around? Where was the little girl who loved playing and sitting on the couch all together as a family? How could that same little one do something like that? We still have a picture of her sitting on the floor looking up at us on the couch with a big smile as if she was happy that we were all together. In a moment, she seemed to have gone from happy and fun to mean and hateful. She became disrespectful and refused to take any direction or do anything she was asked to do. Rebellious? I think, I can with confidence say yes.

We hoped once she had time to deal with whatever she was dealing with, things would return to how they had been. We still had many fun times, but those intense times of rebelliousness were a struggle. I continued to believe that once the dust settled, we would be a wonderful little family.

Issues came up about the new family arrangement. How did the girls fit, how did I fit, and what was going to happen with their father? As before, we continued to encourage their relationship with their father. We continued to talk about how important he was and for them to always love and respect him.

We helped them understand they needed to nurture a relationship with him, and we promised someday they would be glad they did.

The lesson we tried to teach them was that if you didn't work at it, someday you may regret it. To their credit, not without struggles, they did work at it, and they have always kept their father in their lives. It makes us happy to see them now as adults with their father so active in their lives. He has done so many wonderful things for them, things we would never have been able to do.

Getting married seemed to affect us in ways we never imagined, planned for, or were prepared for. We believed getting married would have a positive impact on the girls. We thought they would feel secure and loved and wanted. I think Sarah felt that way, but maybe Megan felt discarded and abandoned. Our marriage also impacted our finances because her alimony stopped. We planned for that and knew it would be difficult but felt it would be well worth the strain. We also needed to decide to either buy out her ex-husband's part of the house or move. However, working out any deal on this house was impossible because it was way out of our price range, not to mention the fact he wasn't particularly cooperative.

We eventually moved into a little two-bedroom condo giving us more time to find a place to make our own. We left a two-story, four-bedroom,

2400-square-foot home, with a neighborhood golf course, in the hills and squeezed into a little one-bathroom, two-bedroom condo. In this case, having little to our name was a blessing. There is another blessing that came along with the condo. We spent a wonderful Easter in that place which seemed to be around the time that Connie became pregnant.

Three months later we bought a great home in the valley that we now called our own. Except for Megan's occasional outbursts, things were going nicely again. After sharing a room in the condo, the girls were excited to have their own rooms. I was told, the four-bedroom ranch was once owned by Disney Studios. The studio often let executives stay in the house during long-term projects. It was nicely landscaped as you would expect for an old Disney home. It was our first home together, and we loved it. Even Megan now seemed content. With this added expense and the reduced contributions from Connie's ex-husband, we took the girls out of the Christian school and put them in a public school just around the corner.

Unpacked and with the rooms all decorated, we could relax. Everything seemed normal and stable, even our tight finances seemed quite bearable.

The girls expressed their unhappiness because they were not spending as much time as they hoped with their father. They would have plans to see him, and sometimes he just didn't show up. They would have plans to be with him for the weekend, and sometimes he would bring them back after spending only a few hours with them. Sometimes he would be good enough to phone and cancel. Broken plans with him continued to be very hard on them and was something they still could not understand. They seemed to always blame themselves for him not visiting. They wondered why he didn't like them or want to be with them. It was hard for us to see them so disappointed, and we explained as best we could that it was not about them. While we did our best to cover for him, I don't think anything can replace a parent who doesn't do what they say they will do.

That part of dealing with the ex-husband was tough on us too. We made plans over and over again, and most of the time our plans had to change because he changed his. Seemingly, we were still hitched to his wagon which impacted much of our lives. He could really do what he wanted, and all we could do was adjust to what he did. In a sense, we were at his mercy. We cancelled plans left and right and learned to sit home just in case things didn't go as planned. Honestly, it made me angry.

I would like to add something about a parent and their commitments with their child. My youngest sister is in her fifties and still speaks of the disappointment and loss of respect she felt for our father well after our parents' divorce. He promised her a pony and never delivered. The pony thing was not a passing fancy for her as some things are for kids. She has a few horses, competes, and has many prize ribbons around her house. Horses are her thing, and that passion has been passed down to two of her daughters who are both very invested in and have competed in the horse world.

If he had followed through, don't you think it would have been the most amazing adventure they would have shared? He really missed some amazing years with her. She also speaks about him not showing up for a date when he said he would and how much that hurt her. We may not understand how such hurts stay with the kids, even forty years or more later.

The thing to be aware of is how important those promises are, and how treasured the time is with the parent who has moved away. We watched the girls get so excited, then see them so beside themselves during those times. The parent may not need the time, but the kids sure do. We spent a lot of time trying to patch up the damage done by something that may seem to be a little thing.

In my years of doing weddings, counseling, and being around kids, I have seen the same thing repeated over and over. I have seen this happen with dads much more that with moms. I am speaking of the parent who leaves, regardless of the reason. It seems they often detach themselves from the family. It makes sense to be detached from the spouse but not the kids. Too often, over time the absent parent becomes more and more distant and less and less a part of their kids' lives. The kids need both parents and want to be told how much they are loved.

I have a friend whose ex-husband continually sends their kids pictures of all the things his "new" family does and has. They get emails with pictures of the new family on their new boat or on some amazing vacation. It seems he continually lets them know what they are missing. That is just plain cruel.

Back to settling into our new home. The excitement about the new baby seemed to unite us and bring us closer. We all had the same thing to be excited about and look forward to. We all were connected by the little one, and she was something no one else had a part in. This little bundle of joy had provided something very big in the lives of our family.

We all had a hand in decorating the baby's room which I think helped us blend into a family even more. We were all participating in something new together that changed how we viewed the family.

Looking forward to the day our family of four would become five filled the house with constant chatter and excitement. We could hardly wait to find out if the baby would be a brother or sister. We had several discussions about who wanted what and why.

A woman who worked in Connie's office building had gypsies in her heritage and performed a gypsy "baby in the tummy" reading by dangling some gypsy stone on a string over Connie's tummy. Her determination was that the baby was a boy. We shall soon see how accurate gypsy readings really are.

The greatly anticipated event was soon to be here. A few days past our one-year anniversary, the newest member of the family was delivered, and it was a girl. The dream I had long ago of a little blonde-haired, blue-eyed daughter was now nestled in my arms. I now had two little blondes and one adult and one little brunette. I was outnumbered four to one. It was crazy awesome, and I loved it.

Welcome to your new home Lizzie.

CHAPTER 7

New Baby, New Home, New State

We walked up the sidewalk between the manicured shrubs and two birch trees. We opened the front door and brought little Lizzie into her first home. She was asleep, so we quietly placed her in her first bed in her first room, in her first home, for the first time. First things make quite an impact on a new dad, like the feeling of having another life to love, protect, and the excitement of being able to teach a little one the basics of life. I was also about to experience being loved in a way I had never experienced. I had great expectations of the wonderful family we would become and of the exciting things we would do. I had great dreams of helping this family become one that all of us would love just as I had when I was a kid. I also had a deep desire to be the "World's Greatest Dad", or at least be given a t-shirt with those words printed across the front of it for a Father's Day gift.

Lizzie's room was a medium blue with dark wood furniture placed functionally around the room. Pictures, poems, and a prayer were chosen with care, and each hung in its proper place. A new way of life had begun.

All three girls were born in California, permitting them all to lay claim to being California girls. I have to say that in times of bragging, I mention my girls are all California Girls. As you know, I always wanted to be a Californian but would only ever be a transplant. The girls could proudly declare they were indeed "California Natives," and this dad would forever be envious of that claim. That being said, I wonder if that would give them the right to have a "California Native" bumper sticker on their car which was so popular back then. How cool would that be?

Sarah and Megan were excited and thrilled to have their new little sister located nearest their rooms to be peeked in on any time they wanted.

Connie was allowed to take a couple months leave from work to recover as well as to keep a watchful eye on Lizzie. At the time, I owned a business and took as much time as needed to help. I spent hours on the couch holding our precious mystery of life. When I wasn't needed to hold Lizzie, I helped the girls with homework, shot some hoops in the backyard, and cooked if need be. Sarah and I developed quite a rivalry playing Horse which became one of our highest priorities. Megan chose coloring as our "bestest" thing to do.

I felt completeness and fulfillment in new ways almost daily. I was and am blessed to have a daughter who is part of me along with the other two girls. Little girls inspire the most amazing feelings in their dad's hearts along with a very special bond. It took me turning 37 years old for the realization of that long-ago dream to become reality. I sat on the couch for hours, letting Lizzie sleep on my chest. I was overcome with the miracle of this tiny human being. I don't understand how families can separate and not spend every minute possible with their kids. I don't think I could ever do that. I am not judging or criticizing, it is just that bond is so strong. I think I could endure most anything to hang on to it. Life had become a time of wonder, miracles, and firsts, and I hoped it would never end.

Seven days later, Christmas was upon us, and what a wonderful Christmas it was. It could only have been better if we had family to share it with. We went to church on Christmas Eve, carefully tuning our ears to quickly respond to any request to see the baby. When we got home, we exchanged a couple of presents and went to bed. You know, so Santa could do his thing.

Christmas Day was fabulous. We got up to sun pouring in through the windows. I opened the patio door allowing the warm air and birds singing to fill the house. Yes, it was another beautiful Southern California day. I did not need snow to make Christmas special. I just love warm air, sunshine, and beaches. I guess I have already mentioned that and should apologize for going on about it. To be clear, have I ever mentioned that I love warm air, beaches, and sunshine? Now this was the way to celebrate all the winter holidays.

Not having to run from family to family had its good side. We casually opened gifts, Connie put the turkey in the oven, and we relaxed. The girls played all day, and Lizzie slept, well I guess I did too. It was incredible to let the kids have time to do whatever they wanted. Sarah and I even went outside and played a couple of games of Horse. The house was filled with a joy and peace that was incredible. There were no arguments and no attitude issues the entire day. It was a day that seemed to show we all had finally found our place and had made a huge step toward becoming the family we all wanted to be. It was one of the best days we have ever had.

At that time, I could not have known that this Christmas would be one of the very few holidays we would share without fighting and screaming and the slamming of doors.

Just after Christmas, Connie's parents came for a visit. As usual, the girls could hardly contain their excitement. They loved having Grandma and Grandpa around, and again our thoughts turned to making a move east. There the girls would have a big family with aunts and uncles and cousins and grandparents. I loved California and could have stayed there forever, but it would be a small sacrifice to give the kids something they would treasure their entire life.

The struggle of getting the girls to spend a weekend with their father was more difficult now because they wanted to be home with the baby. Sadly, he continued to be unpredictable. He continued to plan weekends with the girls and sometimes keep them, sometimes not show up, and sometimes bring them back early. The girls' feelings got hurt every time their plans didn't go as expected. The night before he was to pick them up, they would pack their little backpacks and share their hopes of what they might do for fun. It was very clear they were very excited to spend some special time with him. I can still picture them both sitting on the front step waiting and how the excitement in their eyes faded when the phone rang. It was as if they immediately knew who was calling. When things fell through, we spent a lot of time comforting them and worked hard to find new and fun adventures with which to distract them.

Connie, Lizzie, and I continued to hang around and react to last-minute changes as they happened. We continued to surrender any hopes of being able to go off and do things we wanted to do because of the unpredictable way weekends often went with their father. It was almost like we were on call, and it was not pleasant.

Not everything we did was wonderful and cozy. I must admit that is was tough being the new guy. Attending the girls' school plays and activities, along with their father and his wife was challenging for me. I was often unsure where I fit and at times felt awkward and uncomfortable. He was kind, and his wife was always lovely. However, I was the outsider, and no matter how nice everyone was, I was always aware of holding that position.

I think the original couple never really understand the awkwardness of being the outsider, and how most events are not that pleasant when both parents attend. I felt like the bad guy. I felt as if I was on center stage with everyone around me saying, "He must be the new guy, who invited him?" or "Why is HE here?" Connie continually expected me to be there for things, and I understood and wanted to be. However, she never had any idea how hard it was on me.

Truthfully, I really didn't like hanging with her ex or sharing in things they always used to do. It is a good idea for the spouse bringing the new person into the family and outings, to try to understand his or her feelings and not brush them off as foolish. Connie and I had a couple awkward instances when I was completely out of place, and she could not understand my discomfort nor accept my desire to stay home.

It took a long time before I felt comfortable in such situations. I was always glad when some events were over, and we were back in the car. To make matters worse, I didn't feel particularly good that he was so successful, and I was barely getting by. I could not offer all the things he could and wished I could do better for all of us.

The dynamics of our little gang changed some as Lizzie required much care and attention. I was very careful to do my best to not show any favoritism, so that all the girls would feel equally loved. I tried as hard as I could, but still, I found this beautiful little baby to be so amazing and hard to not just stare at.

Most of the things relating to being a new dad were comfortable and taken in stride. There was one side effect of dad-dom I was never warned about or prepared for. I was caught completely off guard.

It seems once you have a child, your tear ducts become over developed, and your self-control drops hundreds of points. I had officially become a cry baby. It was an old school yard term I thought I had left far behind me. I now cried at movies. What in the incredible world of Walt Disney had happened to me? I was now watching movies I would have never watched a few months ago. Instead of seeing the big screen filled with manly men doing manly things, I was now watching animated films, romantic comedies, and the Hallmark channel. I was watching fairies, talking bears, and movies teaching me about being nice to others. What was happening to me?

The birth of that little one had seemingly repaired any residual damage to my heart caused by my divorces and turned my heart soft again. I once again had tears after many years of not being able to cry at all. Tears had come back into my world in the strangest of places. However, these tears were not brought about by hurt but by the tenderness of life. With Lizzie's birth came a sort of rebirth to my heart.

I am fortunate I didn't have this little girl during one of my previous marriages. I know I could not have handled being away from her for even a day. In the years that were to come, I would have to travel for work. Anytime I was sitting in an airport and heard a little one cry, I immediately would become homesick. Being away for those short business trips was hard, and I now had a better understanding of how Connie felt having to go back to flying after her first two were born.

I think I even might have endured the issues that broke up my previous marriages had she been in my life. This precious little bundle of love could hold anything together. I know I could never walk away and leave this little, innocent one behind.

Watching Lizzie sleeping so peacefully, I could not imagine the role she would play in helping to keep our family together during the challenges headed our way. Who would know by looking at this baby, she would one day do heroic things in our family. It is an understatement to say I treasured every moment with her and still do.

Over time, Megan developed into a skillful agitator and manipulator. She discovered how easy it was to agitate all of us and began to practice that newly-learned skill on a regular basis. She exhibited the life lesson that practice makes perfect; however, we all could have done without what she was practicing.

We often discussed the pleasure she seemed to get from annoying us. We did our best to help her see she was the only one having a good time. Sarah was gentle, loving, and kindhearted and could easily be driven to her wits end. During those times, Sarah would often be near tears while Megan would act like it was very funny. This new development added the role of referee to our list of parental duties. It was another task we would have the opportunity to perform quite frequently.

The thoughts of living near family increased, and my business seemed to be shrinking. That situation made the idea of moving east a more serious consideration. The older of Connie's two younger brothers lived in a beautiful area in Kentucky and said there was plenty of work there. We enjoyed time with his family and thought it might be a good place to take the kids. In Kentucky, we would be close to family there with only a five-hour drive to family in Ohio and a five-hour drive to family in Illinois, perfect.

Connie approached her ex-husband with the idea. The answer was absolutely not. He talked of how important the girls were to him, and that he would never see them, and that was unacceptable.

From my perspective, his lack of spending time with them all the while we lived just a reasonable drive away, coupled with all the cancelled weekends, seemed to tell a different story. We continued to have dialogue on the subject to which he finally agreed. One condition of his agreeing to our move was a huge reduction in his child support payments. I could understand he would not be able to see them as much but could not understand how his financial support of them should be lessened. Through the years, I have talked with several families who experienced the same situation with a similar result. I cannot read into anyone's heart nor understand why anyone would lessen support of their children because they were not nearby.

Off to Kentucky we went. Unknown to any of us, it seems a Yankee had little chance of getting a job in Kentucky, let alone some crazy person from California. Before I even got started, I had two strikes against me which was bluntly expressed to me by a recruiter. I will save you the details, but living there lasted only three months. We moved again, now to Ohio.

We didn't have a place to go and were broke from all the moving and renting expenses. Our situation, coupled with the grace of my mom and her husband, landed us two rooms in my mom's house.

That might sound like a bad situation, but it was quite pleasant. We all got along well, and Mom got to spend a great amount of time with her three granddaughters.

I found a job as a mechanical designer, and after five months, we rented a split-level in the west side suburbs of Cleveland. We picked a town with one of the best school systems, so the girls would get a great education. It was a fabulous day when we moved into our own place, even if we were only renters. The owner of the house said he would apply a portion of the rent to the purchase price of the house if we wanted to buy it later. It seemed like our future just kept getting better.

Connie found a great opportunity near home, Lizzie went off to day care, while Sarah and Megan took the school bus back and forth to school. As was my experience when I was a child, life for us was also becoming very Mr. and Mrs. Cleaver. The Cleaver family gave the world the picture of a normal, stable, all-American family, including mischievous little Beaver. We seemed to be following their example except we had mischievous little Megan, and all was good.

Friendships were made, schoolwork was done at the kitchen table. We found a great church, and sleepovers and birthday parties became normal things. There were dance lessons, town softball games, and holidays with the big family here in Ohio. Nearby, the kids now had one great-grandmother, four grandparents, two uncles, two aunts, and five cousins, with more to come. Within a five-hour drive, they had two more grandparents, three more aunts, three more uncles, and seven cousins. When we talked about getting them a family, we were not kidding. They loved their family but still struggled about not seeing their father often. Summers brought with them long visits back to California to spend time with their father and stepmom. As Sarah grew older, her desire to make the journey to California stopped, leaving Megan to make the trip on her own.

Things went very well for a time, but then Megan began having issues at school. She wouldn't bring her homework home and would get incomplete scores and seemed to not get along well with some of the other students.

At home, she became more difficult to be around and agitated her sisters at every opportunity. She would stand in front of the television when the girls were watching a movie, take the toys away while they were playing with them, and so on. I don't think in her mind she was being mean because she thought these things were funny. Most likely, she thought she was being quite the entertainer, and looking back, I might be able to understand why she didn't understand why she was being scolded. Maybe part of the problem was she thought everything she did was funny not completely understanding how these things could hurt other people's feelings.

Trips we took became marred with arguing and fighting. Putting her in the van with her two sisters for six hours was like giving Megan two prisoners to torture as she saw fit. Anything she could do to annoy them was all fun to her.

Nearly every holiday was ruined by her behavior. One time, we went out of state to one of Connie's brothers' home for a holiday. Megan at times would get out of control as if she was on speed. I tried to calm her down with no success. She then began calling her youngest sister names that were just mean. When I raised my voice to her, the rest of the family turned on me. Some came at me as if I was the meanest person around. You might imagine how I grew to dislike any idea of visiting Connie's family again. They had no idea what we were dealing with and were making judgement calls about me based on no real information. I was doing my best to keep some balance and order for all the girls, but they seemed to think I was singling Megan out. Connie always supported me because she always knew the whole story, but that didn't help me feel welcome around the family.

Part of our problem was most of the family never saw the things that led up to our disciplining Megan. They only saw us make her take a time-out or saw us lecturing her in an attempt to get her to stop and, maybe just maybe, understand what she was doing was hurting someone else. All other people thought they saw was us picking on Megan, and they quickly would come to her defense. I hated that. We never picked on her; in fact, there were so many conflicts with her that we would ignore lots of other things she did. Those other happenings were things the other girls would have never gotten away with. When you have a child that is difficult to deal with, you would never think your family would take a stance against you, but some family members did, and it was hurtful, especially when they found it appropriate to correct you right in from of the child. That is a big no-no in my book.

Megan got to the point she was starting to not respect us as parents or as any type of authority. We would tell her to make her bed, and she would go in her room, shut the door, and lay there for hours, but never make it. I would tell her to help with the dishes, and she would yell back at me. She began to push back at me at every opportunity.

We could not understand where all these behaviors were coming from. Remember, this was the fun, life is a blast little girl.

This aggressive and mean behavior played out on a larger scale following an argument with a girl at school. The day after this argument, she expressed her anger by carrying a butter knife onto the school bus and showed it to the girl. Apparently, the girl went home and told her mother, and the mother called the school. Thankfully, she had not called the police. Of course, the school called Connie, and we had to have a meeting or two with school personnel.

We had no idea why all of this was happening, nor could she explain it. This was not the Megan we knew and loved. This was very bad and a very big deal.

Her unexplainable behavior was escalating in her relationship with her sisters. One time, she told us she had Sarah trapped in her room and covered her mouth, so she couldn't call for us. She also told us there was another time she backed Lizzie into a corner, keeping her trapped in her room, warning her to not call for us. We didn't know anything about either of these episodes until well after the kids were all out on their own.

It seemed as if there was a fight or argument every other day, and it was wearing us out. I quit my job and started a business, making it possible for me to be home to keep an eye on things. That decision brought with it many sacrifices and a huge shortage of money. It didn't take long for the money shortage to attract the attention of bill collectors. Phone call after phone call was someone yelling at us or threatening us. We hadn't been able to pay all our taxes, and at one point, ended up with several tax liens, making life even more unpleasant.

I felt I was under enough pressure with Megan's acting up, let alone the addition of the financial problems. I don't know how I got through some of those days. I am sure any strength I had to get through those days came from God. There were times I wanted to give up. I spent every waking minute worrying and in fear of what would come next. I was even afraid to answer the phone and was not in any condition to listen to more threats from bill collectors. It became a common occurrence for a collector to call and threaten to take me to court when I told them I had nothing left to give. Yet, they continued to threaten me. I was so beaten down and out of options all I could do was tell them to do what they had to do and hang up.

With all that going on, we were still a little family trying to do our best to have some fun. Even Megan had her good moments entertaining us with her silliness and imagination. She has always been very charismatic and the kind of person who drew people in. She was and still is very likable and loves to be the center of attention. One thing about Megan is very clear, she is not and never has been dumb. On the contrary, she is very intelligent. I wished she would have put as much effort into using her mind to create a great life for herself as she did using it to try to annoy all of us.

It was difficult for anyone to believe she was ever any trouble. When she was around other people, she was a perfect child. She was a Shirley Temple type of little girl to those on the outside. You know, charming and entertaining, living in the spotlight, a little sassy here and there, but angelic most of the time. This was not who she was much of the time at home.

Megan loved summertime when she could get away from her mean parents and fly to California to be with her not mean father. Actually, I remember her telling Lizzie that her father was the best father in the world. He was what a father should be, not a mean, awful person like her father who was the worst father ever. Sarah still preferred to pass on the trip and stay home. Sadly, those trips continued to give Megan new information from her father's perspective about the past with which to judge and berate her mom.

While we enjoyed the summer break from fighting, we also dreaded her return home and the fights we knew were to come. Early on, Megan blamed one parent then the other for the divorce, spreading her anger around. Years later she laid most of blame on her mom where it seems to have found a permanent home. Until this period, Megan had always defended her mom. All that being said, it seemed the fights were most always between her and me. As she spent more time in California, we began to see her begin to disrespect her mother and challenge her on a more regular basis which I would not tolerate.

Even though I met Connie, and the family years after the divorce, I was somehow blamed for everyone's unhappiness, and the reason her mom and father were not together. Megan, who had directed the majority of her anger in my direction, had now started to send more and more anger her mother's way.

The lease on our rental home was running out, and we expected to sign a new lease. Surprisingly, the owner advised us he had decided to sell the house instead of renting it again. He also decided that he changed his mind and would not apply any of our rent toward the purchase of the house. That was our agreement, but it was not in writing anywhere. There was no way we could stay there. If I didn't make something happen within 30 days, we would literally be on the street. I couldn't find any acceptable rental in town, and Sarah absolutely refused to change schools. We couldn't blame her for that and searched harder. At wits end, I could almost picture us in a shelter, vacant building, or box somewhere if something didn't happen quickly. I was truly desperate.

I shared our dilemma with person after person, hoping to find a place to stay. Oddly, more than one person told me to talk to a local builder who might be able to help. I reached out to him and described our situation. He offered to build us a home and laid out the generous terms. We agreed, and on a handshake, he began construction. We got a miraculous break from this builder who built us a brand-new home to our design.

We didn't have a down payment, but a family member graciously helped with that. The builder offered to be the bank for five years, at which point, we would have to get a bank loan to pay him off. My business had begun to grow, making it possible for us to refinance with a conventional bank loan in just four years. It was another miracle. The builder even had a small two-bedroom condo we rented until the house was finished.

After three months of tight accommodations in the builder's condo, we moved into our new home. In a way, it replaced the house Connie had in California when I met her. Our new home was a four-bedroom, 2,700-square-foot home close to schools and in a nice area. Much to their delight, each girl again, had her own bedroom. Interestingly, Lizzie was not quite ready for her own room, so Sarah, the ever-protective big sister, shared a room with her for a while. The girls were doing well in school while dance lessons, parties, sleepovers, and softball continued.

Holidays became even more amazing in the new house. Thanksgiving brought family from all over the country to celebrate together. One Thanksgiving we had 40 family members together for a great sit-down dinner. They came from Ohio, Illinois, Kentucky, Indiana, and Maryland. It became a yearly event, and for a time, it was a family tradition, and it was amazing.

The girls had friends and parties to go to, and my business continued to grow. Connie accepted an offer to change jobs, this one only minutes from home.

Owning a business eventually presented the opportunity for me to move the office into the new house. Being at home daily gave me the chance to be mom, dad, peacekeeper, tutor, and emergency person.

I saw all the school plays, attended all the events, and became an honorary mom. It was funny that if any of the moms were out in public, they would greet me and say hello … I was honored to be just another mom. Our blended family seemed to have fused and was becoming a great family even though, at times, we still had to deal with Megan's challenging behavior. Our finances were getting much better, church was fabulous, and we were all active in various ministries. I felt at home in our new place, and we suddenly had become a very happy family. Dreams can come true. Could they and would they last?

CHAPTER 8

False Hope

As time passed, so did the idea that we had made it through all the hard times, and that life was going to be fine. Everyone seemed content but Megan. She continued to wreck holidays, vacations, and family gatherings with her exhibitions of bad behavior. Can you imagine years going by with almost every holiday, family gathering, and trip being ruined by arguments and bad behavior?

One Thanksgiving she brought a boy home from the inner city, introduced him, then disappeared, leaving us trying to make him feel comfortable while trying to get dinner ready for the 34 people there that year. She was gone for over an hour when she finally paraded back in the house. We were told one of the cousins found her out back on the swing set smoking something. She certainly didn't seem to care about anyone other than herself.

Days later when we attempted to explain how what she did was not right, it became another battle. Then there was the discussion about what she had been doing out back, and that was another battle. Megan clearly had an addictive personality, and we were careful to guide her away from foolish things that she could take to harmful levels. Her response to me telling her she was not allowed to do what she was doing was met with something like, "My dad told me it's okay to do that after a tough week." It was another issue to deal with when his advice contradicted what we were trying to do. He was not aware of the day-to-day dealings with Megan, and whatever he did hear was one sided. For him to give advice that contradicted us undermined our efforts to give her some direction.

These battles were usually nothing disastrous, but she just pushed and pushed until she caused a fight someplace with somebody. It appeared no matter how many times I explained how agitating everyone wasn't fun for the person she was picking on, she continued to ignore me as if it was all too hilarious to stop doing.

I was and still am perplexed at how causing that type of stress with those closest to you would be fun. Most families would agree they would want to make life better for the parents and siblings, not worse.

Other kids seemed to know that the right thing is to be kind to others, but Megan showed little concern for whatever she did, right or wrong. The family would sit down to watch television, and she would talk over the TV or change channels doing whatever she could to annoy us. I warned her with my typical warning, "I am warning you to stop it or you will spend the evening in your room." Always giving her three warnings before sending her to solitary in her room. Sometimes she would yell, stating that she didn't have to. Sometimes she would ignore me and continue doing what she was doing. When she responded in such a way, I would stand up which encouraged her to run to her room. That intimidation could only last so long. I had no idea how I would need to respond once that tactic stopped working. She always pushed our buttons and always tested the limits. Again, kid's stuff we hoped would pass with time. Yes, kid's stuff but with an exhausting frequency most families never experience.

Unfortunately, her bad behavior could disrupt the family anytime, morning through evening. Perhaps she believed she was hurting us by tormenting us and not doing her schoolwork because it seemed so important to us. Of course, she only hurt herself. Megan was now difficult to reason with and control. We had homework time at the kitchen table. While the other girls would be doing their work with pride, Megan would spend the time trying not to do anything. One of the typical bantering would be about words. She would not understand a word and ask us what it meant. Our response was that she look it up. Of course, that became an argument. "Why do I have to? Why can't you just tell me? Why don't you look it up? It's your fault I can't finish my homework! If I get an F you made it happen!" And off we would go into yet another senseless, hour-long arguing session which certainly wears you down. It had no point and brought about nothing of value. In the time that we argued, she could have looked up a dozen words, learned how to use the dictionary, understood the meaning of some new words, and maybe even learn a foreign language. As parents, we wanted her to learn and grow and do well. She not only refused to do what she needed to do, she seemed to need to blame us for any possible repercussions that would come from her not doing things and then fight with us about it. I really did not get it. It made absolutely no sense to me. How could anyone be so stubborn and enjoy so much conflict?

When she turned sixteen, we wouldn't let her get her driver's license. We carefully and in detail explained why. We explained we had concerns about how careless she was and how out of control she got when she went off on one of her silly rants. We explained how not being aware nor in control when driving could cause a lot of damage and hurt other people. That decision could be reversed if she would show some concern for others and act responsibly. We told her being responsible included making a habit of getting home on time, doing her homework, showing an interest in doing the right things, and showing some respect for her family. I was fearful that her reckless attitude could get someone hurt when she was behind the wheel. She lived recklessly and never seemed to think about what could happen when she did something foolish. If she was to hurt someone in an accident after we gave her the okay to drive, I imagine we would never be able to forgive ourselves, and we could not take that big of a gamble. No matter how much she yelled and argued about driving, I did not want her to hurt another person or family nor live the rest of her life knowing she hurt or even killed someone.

She hated us for that and argued repeatedly about it but made no effort to do things different. She believed we were just being mean for no reason. She could not understand any of our reasons or concerns about not letting her drive. She could not see how her recklessness and lack of desire to do the right things should keep her from getting behind the wheel. In her mind, it was just another lousy situation that was all our fault. It was just another example of us trying to "control" her. She continued to choose being nothing but a poor victim blaming her horrible life on us, mostly me. It escalated into a world of constant arguing and fighting about it. She unleashed a higher level of disrespect and blatant opposition to any house rules or direction we gave. Her arguments didn't need to be about any particular topic, she appeared ready to argue about anything and everything. It was like a crazy house. Nothing made any sense, she didn't make any sense, and there was no peace to be found.

Getting her up for school became another battleground. She could never get up. We tried to teach her that she wouldn't always have someone around to wake her up. She needed to learn to do things on her own, she was sixteen after all. It didn't matter what examples we offered regarding being responsible and getting out of bed on time, she would not get up. We set alarms, turned on her lights, called to her, and turned the TV up louder, nothing worked. After listening to her alarm for 20 minutes or so, I tried taking the covers off her bed. Then I tried opening the blinds. I tried spritzing her with water. I even resorted to pulling her mattress off her bed with her still on it. Nothing worked.

After weeks of battling over this, we were lost. No matter what we did, it was apparent we could not make her do anything she didn't want to do, which at this point was to get out of bed.

If we were ever lucky enough to wake her, she would scream and yell for us to leave her alone. Now that is a pleasant way we all want to begin our day.

One afternoon, I was putting some things away in her closet and found a mostly empty bottle of alcohol. When I asked her to explain why she had it, she tried to convince me she was keeping it for a friend. I wasn't buying that one. After another great big heated argument, she finally admitted she was drinking in her room after we went to bed. Of course, drinking was out of the question and had to stop. And of course, another big argument was born about how we were horrible parents, and her life was so miserable which was the reason she drank. Years later we found out that she had stopped drinking in her room before bed. What we also found out was that she had replaced her night caps with a morning pick-me-up of drinking at the bus stop while waiting for the school bus. Things continued to get worse.

We finally told her we would no longer wake her up, and that getting up was now her responsibility. She would need to do whatever she needed to do to get up for things. She continued to not get up and missed the bus and school. She even had the guts to tell us we needed to write the school notes lying to them about why she was late or missed school, so she wouldn't get a detention. It was only right we write excuses because it was our fault she slept in. We did not write any such notes, and she did get detentions, which of course, was all our fault. As expected, another huge argument about us being the worst parents ever came into play. She eventually learned to get herself up when the alarm went off but replaced that issue with coming home whenever she wanted, still not doing schoolwork, getting into trouble at school by cutting classes, being in conflict with other students, and even cutting detentions. She was finally categorized as a "troubled child" by her counselors. Connie attended meetings with the school staff trying to find a solution, without success.

Connie was meeting with the school counselors as well as taking Megan to a private counselor. That counselor suggested a program that was in place at several high schools called the I.E.P. or Individual Education Program. He suggested she talk with the school about it. This program removed her from regular classes and placed her in classes with other troubled or problem kids. The expectations of what they accomplished at school was geared to what they estimated each student could accomplish. They were also to meet with the school psychologist. That change made Megan very angry, and she had no problem telling everyone how much she hated her teachers, counselors, school, and of course, us. By the way, she even skipped on her I.E.P. classes.

Her unpleasant actions and rejection of authority were no longer evident just at home but now seemed to have become a way of life wherever she was. Megan blamed everyone else for her troubles, but there were no problems when she was not around.

The overwhelming theme seemed to be, no matter what we did or said, Megan was going to do what Megan was going to do. I asked her in the midst of one of our struggles, why she kept doing things that got her in trouble. Her reply was, she wanted to do whatever she wanted to do, and if she got away with it, she won. On the other hand, if she got caught or got into trouble, it was worth taking the chance. In her assessment of things, it seems she won more times than she lost which must have only encouraged her to not do things differently.

She clearly expressed her greatest wish was for me and Lizzie to go away, making it possible for Megan, Connie, and Sarah to live together again. It was a dream she had no problem sharing with us on a regular basis. With that in mind, it appeared her next attacks were to try to make that happen. Her refusal to do things differently seemed to say she was not going to quit until Lizzie and I were gone. Her explanation of what she wanted gave me an advantage of sorts, I now knew what the goal was.

As time passed, she became completely defiant. Now, when I told her to go to her room, she would just tell me no. When I would stand up, she showed no signs of leaving. I had to walk towards her to get her to move and occasionally, had to give her a swat to encourage her to leave. I understand that last sentence may raise some eyebrows. Let me define what a swat is to me. A swat is an open-handed slap with the palm of the hand. It was never close to full force and was always on the leg or rear. It was always an attention-getter rather than a punishment. In all our years together, I may have swatted Megan a dozen times.

Of course, a swat became child abuse in her stories, and now I was the criminal who supposedly beat her. The story of getting a swat became a story of getting a beating. It is easy to understand how a person claiming to being beaten would attract a great deal more sympathy. That story managed to get all over church causing some to think I had become a horrible parent even though the other girls and I never had any problems. If this supposed constant ill-treatment of Megan had occurred, why then did neither of her sisters ever see any such thing. Add to that no one, anywhere at any time, had ever witnessed Megan being treated badly. True, I may have swatted her a few times in her entire lifetime but never spanked her and certainly never beat her.

As I mentioned before, she was manipulative and charismatic, and when she spun a yarn, everyone believed her. If you didn't believe her, she would keep at you over and over until you did. Her persistence was the technique that made believers of people. In some circles I might imagine it could be thought of as a mild form of brain washing.

Every chance she got, she shared her ever growing tale with people about how I was mean to her. Eventually, it grew to me beating her and then on to me abusing her, and she amassed a small following of believers.

It was hard doing things and going to events when I knew there were those who thought I was horrible to her. It made life a lot less pleasant, feeling I was always under a microscope. It is interesting how people, even friends, accepted the stuff she put out and never came to us to talk with us about it. Even today, if we stop and pay attention to the world around us, it seems people more willingly accept bad things about one another rather than good things.

There was little we could do to change her opinion of us being bad parents. She even claimed sending her to her room was abuse. Not of help to us was her father because according to Megan, he agreed that it was cruel. We came to believe everything we did to curb her actions was considered abuse in her opinion. Whatever she wanted to do but couldn't, was us being abusive. If we did anything but let her run free and wild, we were abusing or controlling her. I don't know where she got such a warped perception of reality, but it was deeply rooted in her.

There was a time her manipulation skills reached a new high catching me completely off guard. For no obvious reason, I noticed a change in Connie. She was distant and seemed to be second-guessing me on a regular basis. I was at home all day. I was the one who made sure homework got done. I did my best to keep the arguing to a minimum and handled any discipline matters, none of which was pleasant for me. Why did she feel the need to second-guess me? She had seen how I dealt with conflict for years with no concerns, but all of a sudden, my ability to be fair was under scrutiny.

On Wednesday evenings, Connie regularly went to church for worship practice while the girls stayed home with me. Apparently for quite a while, Megan had been telling Connie that while she was gone, I had been picking on her, been abusive by locking her in her room, and whatever else she could dream up. Shockingly, Connie had begun to believe her. It all came out during a tense conversation Connie and I had about why she was continually checking on what I had been doing. I agree she should check if she believed I was out of line but talking to me first rather than just believing Megan would have been better from my viewpoint. I was very hurt, Connie was angry, and I was quite angry. It was a matter of trust, and clearly, she didn't trust me. Megan had managed to create a high level of mistrust in Connie and put a nice sized wedge between us. Ouch! Why was I even still here? I wanted to just tell them all, "Fine, you three can have this crumby life you have all to yourselves. I do not need to live like this. I will leave the family. I will end the marriage. I will never be around this craziness ever again." Something inside made me hold back, and I kept my mouth shut and sucked it up.

Megan used her gifts of manipulation and storytelling to get her mom to turn against me. She had successfully pitted us against each other, a job well done. I had been in the front lines, in the middle of all the battles and fights, and continually gave so much of myself to hold everything together, and I was being doubted? I believed I was the only one trying to make this all work.

I did respond, although not in the way I wanted. I told Connie, "Fine!" and I was out of it. I would no longer be responsible for Megan nor her behavior, schoolwork, chores, or anything. If she believed Megan, then she would have to deal with all that stuff, including any needed discipline. I would have no involvement whatsoever with that child. She gladly agreed in a way that stunned me. It was as if she felt she, the "righteous righter of wrongs," was charging in to protect Megan. Meanwhile, I was being thrown to the wolves. Some marriage this was.

With me completely out of the picture concerning anything to do with Megan, it didn't take Connie long to see how she had been manipulated. During the change in authority, I began to have a much better life. I could live the rest of my days never again having to deal with all that junk. She quickly became frustrated and saw the distortions and untruths about all the things she had been told. We both had a discussion with Megan and informed her nothing like that would ever happen again. We learned we needed to check with each other every time something happened to make sure we both had a truthful understanding of what was actually going on. We also would come to an agreement on how any situation would be handled. We agreed we would not take her word for anything until we talked. Again, the other two girls never saw anything Megan claimed to have happened. Happily, that agreement shut the door on any future opportunity for Megan to manipulate us or turn us against each other. Connie asked me to handle most things again, and sadly, I did. Talking and working together was one of the best decisions we had made. It was good that it happened because now we all had the same view of things, and we as parents could stand stronger together. In these kinds of situations, parents must present a united front, leaving no gap for the child to penetrate and do damage.

Looking back, I know parents want to trust each other and know parents want to trust their kids. I also know how we automatically do trust each other. However, in situations such as this, automatically trusting the child was not a good decision. We should have compared notes much sooner. Connie should have come to me long before buying into what she was being told. It was a valuable lesson for both of us.

In an effort to solve the problems we had been living with and in an effort to get Megan help, we began taking her to both Christian and non-Christian counselors. Not to my surprise, she manipulated them all. As I said, she is a very smart person and could completely control any session. We accompanied Megan to her very first session with a Christian counselor. Megan went in while we waited in the lobby. After about thirty minutes, the counselor came out of the session, sat with Connie and me, and immediately attacked and berated me with all sorts of accusations without ever talking to me or Connie to verify Megan's story.

Using that situation as an example, we developed the opinion she confused all the counselors she went to by simply outsmarting them. In fact, years later, she admitted to manipulating some counselors to get a particular medication she wanted. Over the years she abused a variety of medications that we had no idea could be used as a recreational type of drug. This brings up something important for us all in similar situations. As parents with children using medication, we should become informed on the "alternative" uses for prescribed medications and side effects. Some of the drugs she had been given over the years did what they were supposed to, but when she doubled or quadrupled the dosage, she got some kind of high or buzz. One of them she even used as a weight loss pill. Some of them can even be sold and make the kids money. We were not aware of any of that when we were dealing with this and wished we had been wiser and more aware.

She may have thought she was winning in the fight against her mean parents, but in reality, she was hurting herself more than she may have understood. Her behavior with the counselors started her on a path that would eventually lead to unimaginable hardships for her. If she had only been honest and had a real desire for life to change for the better, she might have avoided years of horrible experiences.

She had been diagnosed with ADD, ADHD, bipolar, just being extremely defiant, and borderline personality disorder or any combination of them. Over the years a variety of medications were tried with little results. Some were given with horrible side effects, and no firm diagnosis was made until recently. Some medications affected her so adversely we wondered if she had really lost her mind. It was horrible to watch.

Even so, she seemed amused by all of this and never exhibited any desire to change, accept advice, or get better. She was very much in control of her world but chased everyone away in the meantime. We continued to pray for her every night, leaning on God to help us all in a way that only God could. We were running out of ideas and help. Life was so bad, I hated nearly every moment of it. There was very little joy in our home, but we did the best we could. When there wasn't yelling and screaming, there was a ridiculously high level of tension. Megan constantly watched everything we did for any reason to attack us for being bad parents. We were scrutinized twenty-four hours a day, seven days a week. We owed a good home to Sarah and Lizzie as well as Megan and did what we could to provide some happiness and stability. I felt like I was letting the family down. I desperately wanted all this to change. I wanted to do all I could to fix this mess, but I had no idea how other than to leave. Adding medication into the equation certainly didn't help.

The scary thing about prescribing pills to someone in her condition is that you may never be sure of what they might do with them. The first time there was a pill problem, I was at church for a men's event.

We were planning a men's renewal weekend like the one I attended a year before. That first weekend I attended was one I really wanted to skip, but friends and family pushed me to go. One of the guys even came to pick some of us up in a van to make sure we went.

I always believed in God and acknowledged Christ as Savior and thought I was a fairly good guy. Honestly, I was never as great a person as I thought. I am somewhat embarrassed by how I behaved and how I thought at times. All our struggles since coming back east had caused me to shut down once again. My heart had become hard.

However, that men's weekend changed me from the guy I was to a new person in so many ways. Jesus opened my heart and walked right in. During that weekend, I began a new and deeper relationship with Christ that changed me forever. He was now a part of my life and existence in a way I never imagined. He scrubbed the old scars off my heart and made me whole. I can truly say that weekend was my moment of change. The renewal was when I surrendered to His will as best as I understood it. I wanted what He offered even if I had to let go of the hurt of the past and the sinful desires of the present. It was so precious a gift, I could not let it pass me by. I returned home from that weekend very much renewed.

Please permit me to take a bit of a side road here. Maureen, a wonderful friend who lives in Georgia, read a draft of this writing and asked me when I came to a relationship with Christ. Her question required some thought to answer. I believe I always had a relationship with Christ only in varying degrees. My parents were very involved in church when I was young, so I was always in Sunday school and even in Lutheran school for the sixth, seventh, and eighth grades. In the years after high school, I set my faith and desire for Christ aside to some degree and have seen that many kids do the same thing at that point in life.

What seems to have happened is that my relationship with Christ and how I understood things grew over time along with some supercharged moments. It seemed when I made myself available, God filled me more and more. That renewal weekend and the following fifteen weekends I served on, gave me many of those supercharged growth moments.

I believe much of our growth comes from a personal commitment to learn. Over the years I have read around a hundred books and have done my best to apply some of what I learned to how I lived my life. I was overcome with the desire to learn as much as I could about God, who He is and who I was supposed to be. This eventually drove me to spend a few years attending Bible College. When a person seeks to learn and grow, it happens.

There is another side to that story. Growth and a deepening relationship with Him also came in moments of deepest despair. When things seemed so bad, and nothing I did impacted them in any way, I learned I had to trust

Christ to get us through. The years and struggles with Megan strengthened and deepened my trust and faith in ways a yippee skippee life never could. On the other hand, it seemed like the better life was, the less I may have felt I needed God and maybe even ignored Him. However, the worse life got, the more we talked, and the more our relationship grew. Being an ex-bodybuilder, I use this analogy often. You can't get big and strong watching TV. The only way you can grow is to be in the gym, pressing yourself to new limits. Like they say, "no pain, no gain." Sometimes that phrase applies to life as well - pain can bring gain.

The year after that great men's weekend, I was a member of the team putting the next weekend on. I was at church in a planning meeting with fifteen other men. These meetings regularly lasted anywhere from three to five hours. Connie was at the pastor's house across the street from the church attending a graduation party for one of his sons.

During this time, Sarah, Megan, and Lizzie were at home. Sarah was the big sister and a great babysitter, and we never hand any problem leaving the girls together on their own.

I was completely unaware that a short time into the graduation party, Megan phoned Connie telling her she had deliberately taken too much medication. Connie would give her life for any of the girls, and when she heard what Megan had done, she jumped into Super Mom mode and raced home. How could any mom respond to news like this? It had to have tweaked every nerve in her body and set her mind racing.

Connie got home, grabbed Megan, and rushed her to the hospital. Connie was trying to save her daughter's life, and being patient with the admission process was not something she could afford. While the nurses were taking Megan to the emergency area, they collected as much information from Connie as they could.

When done with that, Connie took a seat until they were ready for her to be with her daughter. Hours had passed, and I was still in the men's meeting with no idea this was going on. After we were well in the meeting, the pastor interrupted and told me Connie was on the church phone for me. This was extremely unusual, and I tightened up quickly wondering what was wrong. Connie explained what had been going on, and everything was being handled. She asked if I would have the men all pray with me for Megan, and that I should stay and finish the meeting. The men and I all prayed for Megan, and when the meeting was over, I went home. Connie was still at the hospital but had stayed in touch with Sarah.

I don't know why Megan overdosed. I still don't think any of us really know why. I don't know what she thought would happen, but what she got was a stomach purging, a tasty charcoal cocktail, and an overnight stay on suicide watch.

Connie said Megan seemed afraid when she admitted taking all those pills, but this was only her first attempted overdose. What was to come was that her fear of the seriousness of taking too many pills seemed to diminish as time passed.

Once the emergency room released her, she was sent to the drug abuse facility next door for a week to receive counseling. That time in confinement was one of the angriest I have ever heard of her being. She angered the staff to the point they called Connie often to ask for her help. They told her they had never had anyone so resistant, manipulative, and mean.

It was so sad. She had turned the place upside down, even turning the other patients who were there against her. Everyone just hated her and wanted her out of there. She was a menace who disrupted meetings and broke rules and created arguments and constantly ran her mouth. No one would miss her after that week was over.

When she returned home, she seemed the same as always. I was afraid to leave her alone because I could never be sure what she might do. I felt I needed to be there to intervene should she get into the mood to bully or agitate her sisters. I could picture her locking her sisters in their rooms or even setting the house on fire. I also could not ignore her recent attempt at taking too much medication and could not give her an opportunity to do that again.

I stayed in the house all day as often as I could, so I would be there to make sure things ran smoothly with little or no incidents of craziness. That decision somewhat grounded me, hurting us financially.

Megan told us over and over how much she hated us and wished we were dead. Children may at times say such things, but she was no ordinary, angry kid who wasn't allowed to go to a party. In her mind, I think she believed she was the worst treated child in Ohio, if not the entire world. Hearing all her constant threats, Connie and I eventually became a little afraid to go to sleep. We were seriously fearful we could be killed while we slept. After the all-out screaming matches, we had many sleepless nights and sometimes woke up surprised we were alive. She had become a terrorist, and we felt like we were the target.

I cannot put into words how horrible it feels to have a member of your family threaten your life and make you afraid in your own home even if you were not sure how seriously to take the threats. Your home is supposed to be your safe and happy place. For us, home had become walls keeping us available to be intimidated, threatened, and even worse if her threats ever became a reality. How could anyone ever know how serious such threats could be? I am sure we could all say, "Surely she wouldn't do such a thing." True, we said similar things. However, deep in the back of our minds, there was a window of doubt that haunted us while also keeping us alert.

At this point, it still seemed as if people were considering her lies to be the truth rather than fabrications. I felt I had been found guilty for doing things that were untrue. I did nothing other than try to give all the girls a decent home while keeping this one girl from ruining her life while robbing us all of happiness. I wanted them to experience the kind of home I grew up in. I no longer expected our family life would be like mine. I only hoped at some point they would have some of what I had.

I think what most people saw was what appeared to be a poor, unhappy Megan and a mean, overbearing, abusive stepdad. You can tell people what struggles you are dealing with and even explain them in great detail. The thing is that if they are not living it, they cannot grasp the severity of it and how life can become so ugly. Even reading this after it has been written does not express the magnitude of what was going on. To be in this type of situation with no help or support was a horrible place for us to be.

Megan got bolder and more daring as evidenced by a call we got at midnight from a church friend. It seems Megan had gone to bed, closed her door, and snuck out her bedroom window. Earlier, while we were all watching television, she opened the garage door, so we wouldn't hear it later when the house would be quiet. She had also taken Connie's car keys from her purse in the kitchen, making stealing the van quite easy. Remember that she had no driver's license nor insurance. She snuck out past city curfew, and drove to a nearby town to hang out with some kids from church.

Following the call from the church friend and Connie's call to the police, Connie drove to the police station in our town. The police instructed her to follow the two police cars to the house where Megan was. The police pulled into the driveway and were met by the police from the other town. Our officers confronted Megan, handcuffed her, put her in their police car, and took her back to the police station. After a long conversation, they turned her over to her mom. The following day we went back to retrieve our van.

We thought and hoped a brush with the police would help her

understand she was going down the wrong path, but what it appeared to do was encourage her. I believe she was beginning to think she could get away with anything. This was the first of two instances where she would end up at our local police station. The second time was when she was caught shoplifting at the local mall. That shoplifting incident landed her some time in jail and a five-year probation. Her defense was that those big stores had plenty of money, and she didn't, so that made it okay to steal. Where did she get this stuff? I had no idea. She was beginning to do things I never thought she had it in her to do.

In response to her being unaffected by the van business and our believing we were having zero impact on her at all, we filed unruly child charges against her. We did so not in retaliation but in a desperate effort to find someone who had enough power to hold her accountable. She needed to learn there were repercussions for such behavior, but she never would because she kept getting away with things. Grounding her, taking privileges away, or giving her room time no longer carried any weight. There was nothing we could do to get her to do the right thing, but we were hopeful maybe a judge could.

We didn't know what to do with her, nor did we know how much more we could handle. We had several talks between us and with Megan about military school. It seemed to produce good results, but even as horrible as life was, we just didn't have the heart to send her to one. We hoped that her taking the car without permission, not having a driver's license nor insurance, and her behaviors would finally get someone in authority's attention. We hoped we would finally get some help with her. We were losing any grip we had on her. She grew in the knowledge there was very little we could do to control her and how little authority we really had over her. She was right, what could we really do? We were coming to the same understanding; we had no ability to hold her accountable.

We went to court and sat while Megan talked to the judge in his chambers. Eerily, memories about our meeting with the Christian counselor came flooding back. This was different. There was no way she could turn this back on us.

Before going to court, but after we learned of her sneaking out to drink, steal the car, and other things, I took the crank off her bedroom window. I did that so she couldn't sneak out again. I also took the door off her room, so it wouldn't be so easy for her to hide in there and drink. We lived in a ranch that had a huge window with a crank just outside her bedroom door.

I figured she was safe, not to mention that the front door was right down the hall. The girls also had their own bathroom, so she could get dressed in there. She was never put in any kind of danger or duress as the judge should clearly see.

The Juvenile Court judge ended his session with Megan, came out, and immediately attacked me. He ordered me to put the crank and door back on. I spoke up to explain why I did what I did, and he harshly told me to shut up, do what I was told, or he would hold me in contempt. The man never heard anything from Connie or me, not one word or explanation. We were crushed and devastated. Our hopes were crushed. If a judge would not support us in our dealings with a child who had broken the law, then who could we turn to? Apparently, we were powerless. Apparently, Megan was in control.

I told you Megan was really, really good. We looked to this man as an authority figure that might help us show her there were consequences to bad behavior, but no, he attacked me. Even breaking laws didn't seem to matter to the guy who was supposed to uphold the law. Why was I bothering with all of this? Life was bad, and now with the judge letting us down, I envisioned it only getting worse. Out of the building and on the way to the car, Megan looked at me and said, "Ha ha, I won!" The war raged on, and she had won a big battle.

Here is something else we learned. As parents, we should have demanded to speak with both the counselor and the judge before Megan did. I am not sure if that would have been possible, but it makes sense. We were the ones taking her to the counselor, and we were the ones pressing unruly child charges. I wish we had realized that giving her the chance to tell her stories before we could provide a clear understanding of what had been going on could rob us of any opportunity to be heard.

"Ha, ha, I won!" What? This was no game. This was not a contest of winning or losing. For Connie and me, these were serious matters that could produce serious consequences. It was about being an upright person, trying to raise a family, giving them as much as we could just as any parent would. We did our best to guide all the girls and give them sound direction. Our efforts proved good for two of the girls, but Megan was another story all together. How it came to the point of keeping score bewildered me. How it came to her against us was even more difficult to understand. Connie and I grew up in families where we cared for one another, where we respected one another, and had each other's back. This was all so absolutely foreign to us. I knew how to function in a family that had each other's best interest in mind. I had no experience in the workings of a family in turmoil, seemingly doomed to failure. I was lost in a place I had never been nor had ever seen.

I was almost embarrassed to show my face around town. She was wining battle after battle and was gaining power with each victory. After each "win" she became bolder, more rebellious, more disrespectful, and more confident. She was so far out of control I found it hard to find much of the real Megan at all. Wasn't anyone else worried this would all lead to more terrible things? Wasn't anyone looking toward the future to see where all this could lead?

The judge also ordered a county social worker to come into our home to check on what we were doing, protect Megan, and evaluate the level of disfunction and or abuse. After my experience with him, I imagine he expected or even hoped the social worker would find Megan's claims to be true, so he could deal with me personally. In my opinion, he missed the boat completely, making me wonder if anyone he dealt with got handled properly. The social worker came in weekly and talked with Megan, the other girls, and then us. Megan may have seen these meetings as the vehicle leading to the final victory making her dream come true. She probably believed she had yet another ally.

Following her frequent, blatant expressions wishing I was not living there anymore, it was easy to believe she hoped the social worker would find me guilty, and either put me in jail or at least kick me out of the house. This process would be interesting to see in action.

In some battles, Megan threatened to call family services on me, telling them I was abusing her. The only response I could come up with was to get the phone and hand it to her saying, "Go ahead, call them. The first thing they will do is remove the child from danger." I don't know if I was right or wrong, but it always shut her up. In any event, her wish had come true. There would be someone from family services in our home weekly, and Megan now had the opportunity to prove the abuse to her.

While these evaluations and meetings were going on, Megan was on medication for whatever disorder of the month she had been diagnosed with. During what was the social worker's last visit, she stated that she saw nothing wrong in the home, that we were good parents, that the girls were safe and in good hands, and would be filing her report to that effect. She evaluated us as competent parents and sternly directed Megan to accept our authority and get under control. Megan's anger could have registered on the Richter Scale. She grabbed her bottle of pills, ran to the bathroom, locked the door, and yelled that she was going to kill herself. Connie and I were horrified, but someone was now actually seeing Megan in action. I banged on the door, asking her to come out to talk; the door remained locked. I then pounded on the door demanding she come out, feeling that time was of the essence. While all of this was going on, the social worker calmly stood nearby watching. I imagine she had witnessed even worse things than this many times.

Finally, Megan unlocked the door and came out with the bottle of pills in her hand. When I saw them, I instinctively knocked the pills from her hand. I did that to prevent her from turning back into the bathroom to repeat the entire scene over again. Her threat had to be taken seriously because of the other overdose. Megan looked to the social worker and started yelling, "See, child abuse, child abuse, he beat me!" The social worker advised her that it was not abuse, and she probably would have done the same thing.

Our case was closed, and Megan had not gotten the results she may have wanted. This loss appeared to have outraged her even more, and things escalated. Being devious and smart, I think my reaction to her running into the bathroom with the pills told her that she now had some newfound power over us. There was absolutely no remorse, but a slowly developing cunning that came out of that episode. Those magic words, threatening to commit suicide, would give her a new weapon.

I felt like I was in the middle of the worst dream ever. Nothing ever changed for the better. Our situation was utterly hopeless. These near daily battles and challenges were killing me. I took more abuse from her than I ever took from anyone. I had given up on my past marriages with far fewer problems than this one. I reminisced, had I stayed in either one, life would have been so much easier and most likely better. Neither of them was nearly as bad as this. I was labeled a creep, and I was often ill from all this nonsense. I was broke again because I had to be in the house as much as possible. I had given up other career opportunities that popped up, such as a national sales manager position. I passed on such things just to be there to keep a watchful eye on daily activities in response to this kid's pledge to get me out. Where was the upside of this relationship?

Others began to understand our financial situation, and it is quite humbling to have someone from the church show up at your door just before Thanksgiving with a food basket and turkey. They also showed up again for Christmas with a food basket and the following Thanksgiving. It was humbling, but we gratefully appreciated their much-needed donation.

I could not live like that anymore. I was done and told Connie it was all over, I quit. I was ready to give Megan her wish, take Lizzie and leave. It would soon be over. I had taken this craziness for too many years and it had to end. The fighting and manipulating never stopped. Yelling, screaming, and threats seemed like a daily occurrence, sometimes a couple times a day. I was worn out. The thought of moving on made me happy. I was in such a bad place, just contemplating being gone made me happy and cheerful. Something was wrong with that.

I wondered how Connie would survive if I was gone. Maybe there would be nothing for her to survive. Maybe if Megan got what she wanted, things would be normal for all of them. I can't tell you how desperate I was. I can't even seem to translate my feelings into words. In fact, as I am writing this, my stomach is churning. My feelings drove me to a place where I didn't have enough strength to worry about anyone but myself.

There is one thing some people don't see or consider. In this case and many others, the parents were being emotionally abused beyond what anyone could imagine. I don't think it ever crosses people's minds that parents can be victims. If I had done and said the things to her that she said to me, I would be in jail no questions asked. This life was certainly nothing I could ever have imagined or wanted. This was certainly not the little band of five eagerly working together to build a wonderful life.

My reputation was messed up, my career had little future, and my health was declining. I couldn't focus on our depleted finances and was depressed. I didn't have much left to lose but my sanity. Once free, maybe I could rebuild my life.

One Saturday afternoon, I was doing chores and catching up on yard work. It was a hot sunny day, and working in the yard we had so carefully planted and landscaped was a joy. People often commented on how it should be on the cover of some magazine. It was a relaxed yard that brought the feel of nature to our door.

I came in the house for some water and heard Megan hollering at the top of her lungs. I followed the sound to our bedroom in the back of the house. I had heard such sounds many times before and was mentally preparing for what I imagined was happening.

I turned the corner in the hall and saw Megan standing just past the doorway shouting and screaming at her mother. I entered the room and saw Connie sitting on the bed looking hopeless and exhausted. When standing, Connie was about five feet four inches and about one hundred and forty pounds. Towering over her in full bullying mode was Megan at five feet ten inches and about one hundred eighty pounds. When Megan was in attack mode, she was certainly intimidating. This is important to comprehend because as I write about what people might interpret to be little Megan, it could be easy to picture a poor, tiny, petite little girl. Also know, at this point, she was seventeen years old.

As I understand it, this argument had been going on for over an hour already. When I say argument, you might envision two people screaming at each other. That was not the norm. Our arguments were typically Connie or me trying to explain as calmly as possible why we had made the decisions we had, which was met with Megan's barrage of words, screaming, and threatening. I stood with my back to the sliding door and did my best to catch up on what had been going on. I had to only hear a few sentences to know where things stood. Megan was furious about us not allowing her to get a driver's license. She battled with Mom trying to verbally beat her into submission in order to get her license.

I heard her calling her mom the worst mom in the world, she was mean and wouldn't let her drive because she hated her, told her that she was no good and shouldn't have children and on and on. I had to come to Connie's defense. This was not even close to the first time Connie had been judged by Megan as being a horrible, incompetent mother. This had to end now.

It was one thing to argue the validity of driving, but to insult and disrespect her mother was what lit me up. I was angry, saw my opportunity, and took it. I could not stand by and witness such disrespect. I yelled at her that it was unacceptable for her to speak to her mother in such a way and to just shut up. I yelled at her that, in no uncertain terms, this was over. I didn't stop the argument but got her to focus her attack on me instead.

I was so upset this time, I joined in a shouting match with Megan. No matter how much I wanted to, I simply could not remain calm and fought back with as much force as she attacked with. How many times did we have to explain why we did not feel good about letting her drive? It was far beyond that. We didn't just not feel good about it, we were afraid to let her drive. We couldn't trust her to make good decisions. We couldn't trust her not to drink or do other stuff. If she was out running around on her own, who would know what she would get into. We couldn't trust her to abide by the limits we set, and we did not believe others on the roads would be safe with her in a car. She could not focus on anything for more than a few minutes, and with a car, the radio blasting, and her lack of ability to focus, not to mention her not having any idea how serious driving was, we could not agree to her driving. It would have been easier to tell her okay, but it was not the right thing to do.

The discussion digressed into her screaming all kinds of nasty things to me, liar, child hater, mean, lousy parent, and then telling me to shut up and mind my own business. Then she turned back to attacking her mom. I yelled at her to stop. She ignored me. I yelled at her a couple more times, and she acted like I wasn't even there. I took a couple steps toward her to swat her backside to stop her attack on her mother. She saw me step toward her and turned sideways, and I missed completely. I attempted to turn her so I could swat her as intended, but she shoved me to the floor.

Let me help you get the physical match up correct. I was one and a half inches taller than her and about thirty pounds heavier. All in all, it was not the horrible mismatch one might think. Sure, if I had been using all my strength, I could have overpowered her but that wasn't what I was trying to do. I wasn't trying to hurt her, I was only trying to stop her abusive talking and end this confrontation. If I didn't make it stop, it could go on for another two hours. It had to be over.

After she knocked me down, I got up and attempted to swat her again and missed again. She shoved me, I shoved back, and we ended up in the laundry room right outside our bedroom door. She was screaming at me, and I was screaming back. Finally, I swatted her a few times on her leg which finally shut her up and got her attention. I told her she lived in our house and she was never to act like that again. I yelled at her about respecting her mom, to forget about driving, and told her to go to her room. That was the end of the discussion.

The entire thing was like a dream sequence in a movie. It was absurd both on her part and mine. This incident is one that you will see referred to in Megan's own words in her online attack on me later in the book.

I did not get married to live like this. I had not taken on a family to live this way. I absolutely hated what just happened. I let her get to me this time. I lost my cool. Usually, I could go, toe-to-toe, with her for hours in verbal battle, but this time she said the cruelest things to her mom ever, and I lost control. Time after time, I wanted to quit. Time after time, I played the move out in my mind. This time my decision was finally made. I told Connie this was too much. I was done and was moving out right then. I went about our bedroom, laying out my things getting ready to pack. Connie tried to talk to me, but I told her to just stop and leave me alone. She went out to the living room, leaving me to pack.

In desperation, Connie called a pastor from our church while I was packing. Before I could get finished, the pastor showed up at our door and came in. We sat and talked for a very, very long time.

He told us he had seen what we had been dealing with these past several years and told me everything I was feeling was to be expected. He told me he understood completely if I left. He said he believed no one would have a problem understanding if I did leave. Finally, it seemed someone saw the truth. Hours went by as he spent time encouraging me to not give up and stick it out. He prayed with us and offered his council anytime we needed it. When all was said and done, I stayed. In my heart I knew it was the right thing to do but maybe not the smartest.

My lousy life went on, with no hope for change. All I could hope for was survival. On any given school day, I would be home in my office working. Whenever I heard the squeal of the school bus brakes signaling that Megan was home, my stomach would immediately fill with pain. I knew that another attack or argument was about to begin. It happened day after day. There would be a day, here and there, that she would come home and seem to feel remorse and want to talk. During those times, we would spend hours talking about the right things and how to be a good person. In those moments I would hope again.

I don't know if any of those conversations did any good, but I hoped so. I never neglected any opportunity to talk with her, hoping something would make sense to her and change life for us all. In any event the situation didn't change.

We knew our lives would change when she turned eighteen because we would lose what little control we had over her. She would then legally be considered an adult and free of us and our rules. I am sure she was already more aware of that than we were and had included that fact in her plans. Our statement to her was something like, "If you want to continue living in our house, you will have to live by our rules like the other girls. We understand when you turn eighteen you can do as you please, and we know there is nothing we can do about it. If you choose not to agree with our rules, you will have to move out and take care of yourself. The choice is yours." I quietly felt like her eighteenth birthday could be the time when we might be set free from all the turmoil and arguing. I was secretly hoping she would decide to move on.

Years later I read an article published in Empowering Parents-Child Behavior Help. It was titled, "When they don't leave at 18" by Kim Abraham

LMSW and Marny Studaker-Cordner LMSW. This article expressed many of our feelings and hopes, although there was also the fear of not having any parental authority over her and what that would bring.

I quote; "There's a calendar date parents of Oppositional Defiant kids often cling to. (A diagnosis that seems to fit quite well but one Megan had never been described as having.) The 18th birthday. That magical day when your child becomes an adult and you are no longer responsible for him - at least not legally. Sure, you'll still be his parent. But things will be different! No more power struggles, disrespect or refusal to follow the rules. No more embarrassment over the way he behaves or the choices he makes. No more feelings of shame, disappointment or anger about the relationship. He'll be an adult and out on his own. If he doesn't like the rules of your house, then he just needs to move out."

It is a great article and one I wish we had come across when we were at this stage with Megan. If you are in the midst of such a struggle, I encourage you to find and read the entire article.

However, that date was still to come, and for us there was more fear of the loss of any and all control rather than looking forward to the freedom it may have brought.

In any event, it seemed she believed someone had to pay for her happy family being broken up. Someone needed to pay for all her unhappiness and miserable life. After all these years, Megan was now rooted in the deepest belief her parents' divorce was all Connie's fault, and she would need to somehow pay. Maybe I needed to pay too because she might be thinking I was keeping her parents from ever getting back together again. That is a guess, but we all knew for sure I was in the way of at least one of her dreams coming true. The one dream we were all well aware of, the one where life again would be just the three of them. I wonder if she ever considered her mom would not let that happen. I wonder if she ever considered her moms' happiness or her sisters for that matter. Her thinking was clearly self-focused with complete disregard for anyone else. In any event, she continued to attack us with all she had. She was judge, jury, and punisher.

I now had been married to Connie longer than Megan's dad had been, how could any of this make sense? Connie had been divorced before I came along, and her father was already happily married. Perhaps she thought if she could wreck us, then she could start working on her father and his wife. Her desire to get rid of me and Lizzie thus putting the three of them back together again appeared to be all that mattered.

It was so sad that so much collateral damage was being done to Sarah and Lizzie. They had been living in a horrible environment all this time and were missing a normal family life.

I talked with Lizzie while I was writing this, to see what she remembered and felt. She alluded to the fact that she didn't know it was not normal. She grew up with all this around her from the start and just accepted it as normal family life. Isn't that terrible? While it is bad, it gives light to how generations of people carry on the same behaviors. Perhaps they don't know any other way of living. Maybe to them, it seems normal like it did to Lizzie.

Lizzie wrote the following; "As I'm writing this for you, it seems so strange how potentially damaging these occurrences could have been to someone who was my age at the time. But, I really feel no emotion about any of it. Maybe just relief that we all came out of it still intact as a family. In my opinion, that in itself is a miracle. At one point, I realized that all I might ever be able to be to Mom's part of the family is the little girl with the problem sister."

Perhaps among all the drama, no one really got to know Lizzie. She feels like a person with no family identity. When one person takes all the attention and control of how a family lives, there is a cost. Someone ended up paying, and to a large degree, Lizzie was that person.

As much as Lizzie didn't think it affected her, a future encounter speaks differently. Megan would eventually move out and make life at home for us somewhat normal. We were at church when someone came up to me and said, "You know today is the first time I have ever seen Lizzie smile." Can you even begin to imagine how shocked I was? I felt horrible. I felt like I had failed Lizzie as her dad. We were under so much pressure and conflict day after day that I had not noticed. How had we not noticed having a non-smiling daughter? I wondered if my desire to marry Connie had cost an innocent person hundreds, if not thousands, of smiles, let alone the happy moments that brought such smiles. How could I have been so selfish?

I had a dream of helping a little broken family rebuild and become a strong healthy family. I had a dream of loving and being loved. I had a dream of being proud of being a great dad and husband. All I had now was a broken dream. Would I ever have anything more? Would Connie, Sarah, and Lizzie ever find life at home to be rich and good? Would Megan ever find life to be good?

CHAPTER 9

Ongoing Challenges

Megan's issues continued to spread beyond family and friends to employers and new acquaintances. I think the following event may be one that made her decision to move out of our house and on to California more appealing.

She was working at a large local grocery store as a cashier. We still had not let her get her driver's license leaving Connie and me to split the duties of getting her to and from work.

While an employee, she had been found to have stolen over six hundred dollars of goods and cigarettes. She was immediately terminated. A condition of her termination without prosecution was she agree to pay the store back. Fortunately for Megan, the store's policy was not to prosecute in such situations due to the high legal costs. Again, the world let her off easy reinforcing the idea she could get away with anything.

A few days passed since the grocery store fired her, and we all got into another giant shouting match. We took a firm stance advising her that stealing was not acceptable behavior for anyone living in our home nor was she to ignore her agreement to pay the store back by leaving Ohio. We drew a line stating that to live with us, such things were to not happen again. We had not forgotten that if we didn't gain control before she turned eighteen, we would not be able to have her live with us and would be forced to tell her to leave.

Our list of unsuccessful attempts to have doctors and even the law support us in this grew. People acknowledged her wrong behavior but chose to feel sorry for her rather than hold her accountable. Her poor, neglected, little girl routine consistently won everyone's heart, setting her free.

Getting caught and signing a paper agreeing to pay the money back in exchange for not being prosecuted was a bit overwhelming for her. I think she was panicking because without a job, she had no idea how to earn the money to pay back the store. We enforced a tighter curfew and made it mandatory that she find a job immediately, so she could fulfill her promise. The freedom she once enjoyed would have to be earned back by adhering to the rules now in place.

Things went well for a few days, then another of the most horrible shouting matches I had ever seen erupted. This time it was between Connie and Megan. Megan was rebelling against the loss of freedom and the stricter rules. She blatantly refused to accept them. Such arguments often moved from room to room as whoever Megan was arguing with attempted to get away from her. In this case, Connie had said all that needed to be said and attempted to move on. Megan would never let that happen. She would not accept no and relentlessly badgered Connie in every room until they ended up in Megan's room. It got so abusive and hurtful that Connie came into the kitchen and told me to take Lizzie and leave. She was worried that Lizzie would be affected horribly by such a scene. Once I was confident that Connie would be safe, I left with Lizzie.

Connie told me she went back to Megan's room and basically told her what was in place would stay in place, and there would be no deviation as long as she lived with us. Connie told her that was the end of the discussion, and she left Megan in her room. Within seconds, Megan went ballistic and began trashing her room. She went on a rampage, throwing everything she could find. Megan was on a roll, screaming that she hated us. Screaming things that didn't even make sense. Connie heard the ruckus and could not ignore her any longer. She went back to Megan's room and did everything she could to calm Megan down but to no avail. Connie said Megan was so crazed she thought Megan had lost her mind. Connie also told me she felt as if she was in the presence of evil, and that Megan acted as if she had been taken over by some dark force. Even her eyes looked crazed and appeared red to Connie.

Connie finally warned her that if she didn't stop, she would have to call 911. Megan continued to rage, telling her they would take Connie away for being an abusive mother. Connie pleaded, and Megan dared her to make the call.

Connie made the call, 911 sent the all too familiar local rescue team from the fire department. As always, they arrived quickly and must have wondered what craziness they would walk into this time. Connie described what had been going on, how Megan was more out of control than ever, and seemed evil, making all kinds of threats and had trashed her room. Connie added there could be a possibility Megan had taken something or maybe her mind had finally just snapped. She wanted her taken to the hospital for an evaluation.

The rescue squad went to Megan's room to talk to her. Within a few minutes, they came back reporting, Megan was calm, said none of the things Connie told them had happened, and her room was in fine order. Megan also told them she was eighteen. The rescue squad advised Connie if she was eighteen, there was nothing they could do unless she agreed to go. Obviously, she cleaned her room and calmed herself down while Connie was waiting for the rescue squad. It was just such situations as this when she could quickly make herself act normal. Such radical transformations always caused us all to wonder how much of it was an act. Episodes such as these could cause people around us to wonder if we were the mean, conniving parents she tried to convince everyone we were or that maybe we were just crazy.

That outburst was a glimpse into the feared future I mentioned before. How were we supposed to deal with any of this once she turned eighteen? She had to know eighteen was the magic number that took away any lingering control we had over her. If she had been eighteen, the rescue squad would have been legally bound to leave. That victory would have given her the opportunity to continue being abusive toward her mom. Connie's reply to them was that Megan was seventeen and lying.

This was a perfect example of Megan's ability to flip the behavior switch and mislead people. Instantly, all the rage about not having her own way and not being allowed to do what she wanted was gone as if it never happened. Then when confronted with authority, she skillfully lied to make it all go away just like with the counselors and the judge.

The rescue squad did take her to the hospital for evaluation while Connie followed in our car. The evaluation lasted about four hours which resulted in them saying she was fine, and they released her. Unfortunately, the outcome was completely predictable. Again, Connie hoped that someone would see through all of this, get Megan help, and get us help. Megan won yet another power struggle. I have recounted the events of that evening in a few sentences making it seem like it only lasted a short period of time, but the truth is that episode lasted close to ten hours. When I write about our battles, they might not be what most people envision. It was not a typical, "Why can't I do that?...Fine I hate you...then go to your room!" kind of thing. Our battles were never conversations but rather were filled with screaming and shouting and accusations. There were very few conflicts that were counted in minutes because most of them lasted anywhere from two to five hours. It was absolutely exhausting.

Leaving the hospital with Connie, Megan's fury was evident but in control. When they got home, Megan went to her room and called her father. Connie called me, and I came home with Lizzie. That night was the episode that led to the end of her living with us.

Her conversation with her father detailed how mean we had been, and that she couldn't take it anymore. She was now ready to live with him.

I am not sure if he paid the grocery store debt for her or if she skipped on it. I likewise don't know whose idea it was for her to move to California at that time. I wonder if he thought he could do better with her, considering the years of her telling him we were such awful parents. The way she described us as parents and how horrible her life was, would make anyone think they could easily do better. Perhaps her father hoped that a new home would help her settle down. In all truthfulness, I hoped he could do better. If he could, maybe we all could have normal lives after all. If he was wrong, then her poor father could expect some terrible days ahead for both him and his wife.

If people around us could not believe it was as bad as we said, I imagine it must have been even harder for her father to believe. The only way he, or anyone else, could believe it would be to see it firsthand.

The timing of that move to California had her still in high school with only a short time before her eighteenth birthday. She was going to be victorious in her refusal to live by our standards even if she had to move to win. Her last act of defiance was to pack and leave - with attitude. The move would not be horribly difficult for her because she had visited California several summers and some holidays, and they talked a lot on the phone. I imagine she believed anything would be better, and she looked forward to it. Maybe she believed she could control her father better.

The first week in February, Megan transferred from her Ohio high school to the local California high school, making her eligible to graduate. She settled in fine, started going to school, and making all the right choices. We heard she was even doing her homework. To anyone watching, it appeared she was just another normal kid doing normal things. It wasn't long before her father took her to get her California driver's license. If she were to ever move back to Ohio, she could easily drive to the license bureau and trade her California license for an Ohio one. Even if she hadn't gotten one in California, she was now eighteen, and there would be nothing we could do to prevent her from also getting one here.

To an outsider it would seem Megan was right about us all along. One could easily support her and now believe we were the problem and truly lousy parents because now she was normal. Why would a kid who was now so normal behave so horribly around us? Can a person switch disorders on and off at will? None of this made any sense.

The good news was that it was now peaceful in our home. Life was normal for us, and we all hoped that she had found a new life with her father. No one out there knew her history, no one had seen her in action, so she would get a second chance to be happy, good for her. If it went well, we too would get a second chance, good for us. I felt like we deserved that chance for we had paid a huge price to get it.

With things going so smoothly, her father and stepmom must have wondered what all the commotion in Ohio was about. They would have no choice but to believe we were guilty as charged (maybe more accurately, that I was guilty), and that Megan had truly been a victim of our horrible parenting.

Time passed, and all of us believed we were finally getting the normal lives we deserved and hoped for. However, as one might expect, it wasn't long before similar problems started in California. Megan didn't want to go to school, didn't care if she ever graduated, and was starting to become defiant and argumentative. I was told, her father had to write her last paper so she could graduate. He would do what needed to be done so she could finish high school and graduate, and graduate she did.

Megan's father called often to update us on her progress or lack of progress. Watching her behavior creep back to the way it had been with us caused me to feel sorry for her father and his wife. Selfishly, I must admit, I was glad to be out of the storm. I absolutely did not miss having her in our home. I was also glad the truth about us was being revealed to Megan's father by her very own actions and words.

Sarah had moved away to college two years earlier leaving Connie, Lizzie, and me at home. The three of us lived with a newfound calm and peace in our house that we did not often have before. We had no conflict, no arguing, no manipulating or agitating. We had become the loving family I had always hoped for. There were no awful stories to tell, no police involvement, no courts or hospitals, no overdosing or rescue squads. No threats or even the slightest bit of anger. So, this was how life could be? Wow.

We were experiencing what Connie and I had experienced as children ourselves. Every day was filled with joy and peace. We talked and played and grew together. It seemed the fighting had dominated so much of our lives we kind of had to meet Sarah and Lizzie all over again. That last sentence is so sad, thinking that the innocent ones in all this grew up with their parents missing some important parts of their lives.

Months passed, and our new lifestyle had become an everyday thing. We could easily accept the untrue reputation of being lousy parents for the peace and happiness that filled our days. We grew closer together and had not one complaint. The girls were both doing very well and so were we. I was so glad I had not left, for now I could see how we could move forward toward the life we all wanted.

Unfortunately, phone calls started coming our way. Megan called and now complained about her father and his wife. Having lived with them for a while, they had now become the bad guys. She talked of how unfair they were and how she hated it there. She would ply us with her newfound revelation that we were indeed great parents. We were told how much happier she had been in Ohio. She craftily let us know how much she wished she still lived with us. Liking Ohio or California better and who the better parents were changed day by day. It seemed the quality of our parenting depended on who she was angry with on any given day or who she could manipulate better.

Things out west got worse. They argued more often, and she pleaded with us more. When she explained the situations to us, I could see her pattern of agitating and pouring fuel on fires. She could drive anyone to do whatever she wanted just to shut her up. Once a barrage of pleading started, she would not quit until she got what she set out to get. Most of what she did and said made no sense. Her ideas, beliefs, and standards were not normal. It was as if we all spoke different languages.

One such scene played out with her stepmom. She made her stepmom so angry that she flung the vacuum cleaner in Megan's direction. Anyone who tried to make sense of her ramblings could be driven to that point quickly. Being the fine citizen she was, Megan promptly called the police, accusing her stepmom of being violent. That accusation got her stepmom an evening in jail and potentially some minor charges.

Part of me feels vindicated because the same problems we lived with were now happening in California. The only common denominator was Megan. It sounds like fiction doesn't it? Reliving it seems too bizarre to be true, but it is. If you were to hear her ranting, raving, and screaming, you could only conclude she was near insane. It was those times of ranting, raving, and screaming when we often felt we were face-to-face with something evil. It is horrible to even think such a thing about your child, but it seemed to fit.

As anyone could understand, that little battle outraged her father, and within a couple months, he had had enough. He made her pack her bags, gave her some money for a motel, and dropped her off in the motel parking lot. This was the story according to Megan. To this day, we've never had any conversation with him about it, so we cannot be completely sure how accurate it is or if it actually happened. Over all these years, our experience has been accuracy is not one of her best traits.

The story goes that her father had given her enough money for food and a room in a motel for a couple weeks. During that time, she would have to find a job and take care of herself.

We will never know how hard she tried, but she didn't get a job and ran out of money. She soon found herself wandering the streets. She found space in a shed behind someone's house. There she was able to hide her bags and come and go without detection. During the day, she walked the streets and at night would sleep in the shed. This went on for a while until she met a gang of guys. They took her in, and it wasn't long before she fell for one of them.

I am not sure what happened during the time she was with them, but the adventure ended with her calling her mom in a panic, afraid for her life. This would not be the last time she would call for help, telling us her life was in danger. She had run away from them but had absolutely no where to go. She claimed the leader of the gang, whom she had fallen in love with, was threatening to kill her. Her explanation about what happened was so irrational that Connie believed she needed professional help. Megan begged and pleaded to come to Ohio. However, in her condition, help seemed to be needed quickly.

Again, I never remember her showing any regret or remorse. I don't remember her ever apologizing for what she put people through. I do remember her telling these chilling tales but never being bothered so much that she cried. So many of these situations came across as calculated plans to get what she wanted. Planned or not, this time she was not going to get a quick trip back east. She would have to get evaluated first.

Connie called around that area of California and found a treatment center willing to take her in and evaluate her. Connie explained the facility felt Megan was unstable and offered to help her get healthy. Being past the magic age of eighteen, Megan would have to agree, and I believe she would do whatever had to be done to get back to Ohio. With great reluctance, she agreed and was admitted. I wonder if the only real reason she agreed was that she had nowhere else to go. Megan's father picked her up and took her to the facility, and we all breathed a sigh of relief. Whatever her condition, unstable or potential murder victim, she was safe and with professionals who could help, hopefully.

Part of her being picked up by her father was that she agreed to spend the needed time in the facility to help herself. All of us hoped, this time, psychologists would agree on what was wrong. She was evaluated many times while living in Ohio, but no two evaluations agreed. This time, she spent ten days in the facility. At the end of which they felt the need to heavily medicate her.

When we say heavily medicated, she really was. She was calm and peaceful but also numb and resembling very little of herself. It was almost scary, but we were told it would take time for her to adjust to the medicine. When Connie talked to her on the phone, she barely recognized her. Connie was sure she was too medicated. She was diagnosed with bipolar and borderline personality disorder. This was not the first "we are sure" diagnosis we had gotten in all these years. We hoped this diagnosis was indeed correct which would make all our lives much, much better.

When she was released, Megan's father called and advised us he was picking her up and taking her directly to the airport. He told us she would be arriving at an airport in Chicago just in time for Connie's parents' fiftieth wedding anniversary party.

It was not a happy moment for me. She was gone less than seven months. During that time, her father had been the recipient of all the chaos, confusion, anger, and cost. I could understand how he must have felt as I had been dealing with it for years. He was overwhelmed and couldn't seem to take the stress or maybe just didn't want to. I couldn't bear the thought of the return of all that potential craziness, but I literally had no choice.

All that being said, time would tell if the doctors finally figured out what the problem was and had properly medicated her. The old thought to save myself and Lizzie ran through my mind several times before we left for the airport, but we hung in there. After having peace and happiness in our home those months, I did not want it to end for any of us, ever.

We made an agreement with Megan that moving to Ohio would also include her having her first apartment. Megan, her dad, Connie, and I all agreed. Her father helped with the rent and expenses while we would find a place close to our home, and we committed to be there to support Megan and be of any help we could.

I think she really wanted to live with us again, but the rules and watchful eyes were not something she could handle. With the new medication, she seemed to be acting and thinking clearly. We hoped it would all work out, but we would have to wait to see. As it turned out, the wait would not be a long one.

We found a small apartment at the end of our street which was about a mile from our house. This worked out great because she could feel safe and close if she needed us. We managed to find used furniture from family and friends, along with things we weren't using and made a cute little place for her. We occasionally shared a meal together at our house, and things seemed better, maybe normal. My wishful thinking that things were going to be good was not to be.

Three months passed, and things were out of control again. She started drinking and doing who knows what and with who knew who. She overdosed again, but thankfully, she called a friend and told him what she had done. He kept her on the line and called 911 from another phone. He kept talking with her to keep her busy and awake until help arrived. 911 sent the rescue squad from near our house again. They must have thought we were the craziest family around. These guys knew more about us than our family did and were most likely more familiar with us than any other family in town.

They took her to the hospital and into emergency. The hospital contacted Connie, telling her Megan said she really didn't overdose. Connie told them of her past, convincing them it was a good possibility she was lying. When they got back to check on her, she was completely out of it. Because Megan did not tell them the truth, it was too late to pump her stomach. All they could do was put her in intensive care and watch her closely. She remained in intensive care for three days until they were sure all the drugs were out of her system.

Literally days before this happened, Sarah, who had been away at college for three years now, announced her plans to get married. Sarah was living two hours from home which required Connie to help plan the wedding and do most of the leg work here. It was in the midst of selecting caterers, halls, and all the other things that were needed for the wedding that Connie had this drama dumped in her lap.

Planning the wedding and now dealing with Megan's issues was pushing Connie beyond her limits. She was out of energy and cried often. I was afraid she was going to end up in the hospital from all the stress.

While Sarah needed help, the urgent job of finding help for Megan put Connie on very thin ice mentally and emotionally. Making it more difficult, the medical people she needed to talk with seemed to only be available on weekdays. Having only weekdays to do her research forced her to make calls from work.

Connie wasn't aware of this, but one of the other girls was keeping tabs on her and reporting to her boss. With the knowledge of Connie's phone activity, her boss fired her. This was the only time Connie had issues any place she was employed. With our less than abundant finances, Connie pleaded to keep her job and told her boss she was virtually trying to save her daughter's life. The reply was that it was not their problem and deep into financial woes we fell.

Megan was released and went back to her apartment. Before any of us could catch our breath, Megan's landlord phoned telling us they had no choice but to evict her. Can you imagine the level of panic that we felt? We were still struggling with money, Connie lost her job, and now we might be in a position to have to pay for all the fees, damages, and leftover rent payments according to the lease because of Megan being evicted. We signed the lease, and we would be the ones held responsible. Would this stuff ever end? I was so burdened I could not stand it. Yet, somehow, we kept putting one foot in front of the other. I don't know how we kept from losing it. Either we were too stupid to know when to throw in the towel, or it was God giving us strength to not give up. It just had to be God.

When we leased the apartment, we explained Megan's situation and problems to the building managers. As it turned out, this ending was not a complete surprise to them. They told us how they looked the other way several times, tried to help, and were as patient as they could be, but something had to be done. They were great people, caring, forgiving, and sincerely concerned. They are counted among the few who saw Megan in action and believed us as well as doing what they could to help.

They explained how the police had been to her place several times over those few months. Tenants were complaining about loud noise and people running all over the property. Megan had taken a pot and built a fire in it in the middle of the living room and melted the carpet. There were damaged walls and other issues. The landlord said she had tried to work with Megan, but she wouldn't cooperate. They finally reached the point they could not accept her lifestyle any longer, and we had to remove her immediately.

The blessing in all of this was that the property managers did care and believed us to be good people, so we incurred no charges. None. Whoever heard of anything like that? No fee for breaking the lease. No charges for wrecked carpeting nor for damaged walls. Nothing. At a time when things were so desperate financially, we were afraid this would be the thing that would finally push us into bankruptcy. Instead, it came across as a huge blessing. God had our back on this one for sure.

Megan quickly found apartment number two which was the top half of a duplex about twenty minutes from us. I can't remember why, but her life there was short lived. I do remember I was instructed to pick up some belongings she had not been able to pack into her car and was advised the place still needed to be cleaned. We went back to pack the rest of it only to find some of her things in the garage and some of the furniture in the back yard soaked from the rain. We did what we could, cleaned, and left what the landlord had so foolishly tossed in the backyard for him to deal with.

We finished moving her, stored what was left of her furniture in our garage, and she was back in her old room in our house. I was sure this would never be over, and I would be living the rest of my life this way. None of it was normal. None of it made sense. It was an absolute nightmare. No matter what we did we could not get away from it. It was a feeling of being trapped in a world we had no control of. We were trapped in another person's life, and there was no way out. Isn't there anyone who can help? We desperately needed answers and solutions, but all we could do was keep living in this mess.

Bill Murray starred in a movie titled, *Ground Hog Day*. Every time Bill woke up, it was the same day. He had to live that day over and over and over. That is somewhat how it felt in our life. It was the same stuff over and over and over. If it did change at all, it changed for the worse, never for the better.

We regrouped trying to figure out what to do next. My head was reeling, the house was filled with crisis and stress, and the whole family was again in disorder. She lied so well and so often it became more and more difficult to know when she was telling the truth. We prayed often that someone or something would come along to guide her toward a better life or just snap her out of whatever was going on. How long must we watch this once happy, fun-loving little girl live as a person who seemed to have come from another planet? She was so out of control that I really believed she would never make it to her twenty-first birthday. I feared one day we would get a call telling us they found her dead somewhere.

Her adventures were wearing down the entire family. It was as if we had followed Alice down the rabbit hole into some crazy world. I was no Mad Hatter, but I may have been becoming mad. Again, conflict had nearly become an everyday thing. There seemed to be no way we could have one normal day. We were desperate for the kind of day that many people take for granted. We were so desperate. We prayed with all our hearts for just one normal day.

Connie began dispensing Megan's medications for obvious safety reasons, giving her only one dose at a time. To date, there had been two overdoses, one suicide threat, and a variety of threats yet to come.

We made plans to move forward hoping nothing else would happen. When life is like that, you function on automatic while being drained of all your energy and strength. Having her back in the house and remembering how violent and angry she could become, we were again afraid to fall completely asleep. Was this pattern one that we would live with the rest of our lives? Would we ever be able to sleep with both eyes closed? Could we find her a place not with us where she would be happy and content?

We learned that when we got to the end of the rope, somehow, we were given more rope, and we hung on.

CHAPTER 10

Crazy

As I mentioned before, during those few months she was in California, we all had a taste of what a normal family could feel like. I saw how caring and loving we could be. We enjoyed everything together. It was amazing. I saw the family I thought we could have when Connie and I married was possible for four out of five of us. I was very sad it ended so quickly.

Here I was, again in Wonderland, chasing that illusive white rabbit. This was no fairy tale, and I was not going to any tea party, but it was just as crazy. I was out of ideas and energy. I was angry, felt I had been robbed, and felt I didn't deserve any of this. Making matters worse, she was not my kid. Once my anger and frustration calmed, I always came back to understand if I didn't keep fighting for this family, who would? I had to, even if I didn't want to. At this point, it was not some noble decision, I honestly felt like I had no choice.

As much as Megan infuriated us, we loved her. I can't say I liked her though. Honestly, I didn't like her at all. I was tired of all this stupidity. I didn't wish her harm. I did want her to have a decent life. I wanted us all to have a decent life. So far, none of us got what we wanted, including Megan. We had seen what a good and decent family life was like when Connie and I were kids. Why couldn't we have what seemed so normal to us? Why couldn't we give our kids what we had been so blessed to have? Years later, Megan would even attack Connie's home life while she was growing up. She was sure there was abuse in her home which is why Connie was such a horrible mother. She continually told Connie there were dark secrets in her family while she was growing up, and she was just ignoring them. Megan insisted she knew things Connie didn't know because she had seen and heard the signs. Who knows where those thoughts came from? Connie has always talked of her awesome and amazing family life. Abuse? Really?

We tried to give Megan simple, sound advice that would help her calm down and have a real and good life. She never took our advice. She took advice from friends, TV shows, people in bars and at bus stops, but never us. I was dumbfounded most of all by the fact she would accept advice from anyone on the street yet ignore any advice we offered. Who does that? Here we were, people who loved her, prayed continually for her, cared for her well-being, and bailed her out of one situation after another, yet she would not listen to anything we said. As I look back, if she had accepted one or two things we had said, her life may have gone a completely different direction.

Again, we searched, taking her from place to place, looking at apartments. Honestly, I was more interested in finding her an apartment in sunny California than Ohio. Unfortunately, we were not in a position to pop for a several-hundred-dollar airline ticket and send her back in the same way Megan's father sent her to us. That was just another part of feeling trapped. We had no resources to change anything. All we could do was get up the next day, wash off all the garbage, and try again. Day after day, after day, after day.

True to form, when she needed help to get something she wanted, she was as sweet as can be. We knew she could be a great person because we saw it from time to time. We got another good look at the normal kid during the apartment hunt. If only she would just settle into that good, calm person she could be, life would be great for us all but mostly for her.

She found a little apartment closer to downtown. Again, her father subsidized her move in requirements. She got the utilities and phone turned on. Leaving me the final task of packing up our garage and moving her in, again. This would now be the third time I had loaded my truck with her belongings. Only this time it required a longer drive and a tough tiny old hallway that challenged my moving skills. Being her moving and cleanup crew was really getting old.

Living far from our home meant she needed a car, and against my better judgement, I cosigned for her. She had all that she needed, and it was really very nice and something most people her age would be proud of.

She got another job at a different grocery store. This one was very close to her apartment which helped keep her gas budget to a minimum. The grocery store she had stolen from had not pressed charges, so her theft didn't show up on her record. That fortunate break opened the door for this opportunity.

She met a girl who lived nearby with her mom. She was a little younger, but she was very sweet and innocent. She loved her mom and did her best at everything she did. She and Megan became good friends doing everything they could think of together.

We hoped Megan would see the way her new friend lived and how she respected her mom. We hoped that this friend would be a good influence, showing Megan how doing the right things would lead to good results. Sadly, the influencing went the opposite way, and this girl got crazy with Megan. She started drinking, going to clubs, and who knows what else. She began fighting with her mother to the point that she was told she could not see Megan anymore. I think that story ended with the girl moving away from her mom. We felt terrible that this naive, unsuspecting girl had met Megan and how that relationship so negatively affected her life and family.

Again, we moved Megan. Now on to new apartment number four, but that was after one bright moment. She wasn't evicted, running for her life, or out of money. Yay! The new place was big with many windows and high ceilings. When we finished moving her in, it looked good. This was a conscious decision she made because she wanted to live in a nicer area. We had just experienced a fairly normal time, and it seemed she was thinking things through. She seemed to have begun having normal desires, hopes, and dreams. The move went nicely, and we all felt good about pretty much everything.

However, Megan had a knack for finding all the wrong people. Something similar to a magnet finding metal. She was now developing a network of people from a variety of countries with all kind of crazy ideas about how to make it in America. She settled in with a group who were originally from Morocco and spent all her free time with them. She was learning a new language and a new culture which was very exciting to her.

Soon Megan was out of control again. We never knew where these 180-degree changes came from or why. They often just appeared, seemingly with no reason or warning. She started phoning us at two and three in the morning, hysterical about a variety of things. Someone would be chasing her, she would be lost, out of gas in the ghetto, or whatever drama she could find. This happened off and on for years. Even now, years later, when she wants to annoy us, she will call repeatedly in the early morning. At times, validated by our cell carrier, she has called thirty plus times in a row. To this day, I jump and go into sweats when the phone rings late at night.

One of those early morning calls was again emotional. It seems she had invited some guys over to hang and one would not leave. She told me that one guy was asleep and begged me to come down and get him to leave.

I had no idea who this guy was, if he had a weapon, or if he was some big bad dude that could seriously hurt me. This guy could be high or drunk, and I could be walking into just about anything. I remember when I lived in California dealing with a guy in the gym on PCP. There was no way to win a fight with someone on that stuff. I hoped that would not be the case today.

Even with all the things she had put us through, I wanted her life to get on track. I was tired of all this garbage and wanted her to leave us alone. If you would have asked Megan about us loving her, she would tell you we were lying. We all loved her and had all gone so far out of our way and given up so much to help in ways she would never know or understand. But of course, in her mind, we never loved her. If we loved her, we would let her do anything and everything she wanted. If we loved her, we would praise her for the wonderful life she was building for herself. If we loved her, Lizzie and I would just leave already. That is more how I saw her defining love. One thing was obvious, she seemed to never see anything I did, from moving her place to place to now kicking a guy out of her apartment, as an expression of love.

I agreed to evict the sleeping homesteader and made the forty-minute drive to her place. When she opened the door, she looked odd, it seemed she was really afraid. Whatever the reason, the look I saw was the first time I had ever seen her like that. Maybe the trip would be worth it after all. I must admit it knocked me a little off balance. If she looked afraid, what was I going to have to deal with? I went into her apartment and pulled the covers off the guy, and in my toughest guy voice, I told him to take a hike. My words were something like, "Good morning Sunshine, time to pack it up and get out!" I must say I thought my opening line was creative, colorful, and intimidating. Maybe even a little Clint Eastwood or Bruce Willis. As he rubbed his eyes, I waited for his response. He asked me who I thought I was, and I responded that he really didn't want to know, and it would be in his very best interest to be gone as quickly as possible. Out the door he ran carrying his shoes with only one arm in a sleeve in his shirt. The next thing I did was take a deep sigh.

Having to toss a guy out of one of your kids' apartment is a very uncomfortable thing to do. When I think of the things she made me do for her, I can't believe I did them. I really was sick of her nonsense and was not growing any fonder of her. Maybe it was adrenaline or just the old parent protecting his young that made me come off mean to the guy. Whatever it was, I hated having to do such things. I am not a mean nor aggressive person, except for that year or two when I played flag football. Now that was different. Truthfully, being forced into such situations really stunk. Many years later, Megan told me more about why that guy had been in her apartment. Apparently she wanted to get high and they had some stuff to help with that, so she invited them over. As the evening went on, one of the guys forcefully took advantage of her while the other guy restrained her. What an awful, awful thing she had held in for so long.

The craziness continued with Megan getting arrested for stealing from another huge store chain. This time she went to jail. In a way, we were happy that someone finally made her feel the consequences of her actions. She begged us to bail her out, but we felt now was the time to make her sit. Being in jail would give her time to reflect and think. She might even look at the repercussions of her actions and decide that things like stealing just weren't worth it. We could hope, but that is not how it went.

Rather than ponder her situation, she began using the plastic eating utensils to carve tattoos in her leg. Not a day went by that she didn't phone "demanding" we bail her out. We are often told to pick our battles, and this was one we would not budge on. As they say, "Do the crime, do the time."

When she was released, she didn't seem to be sorry for what she did but was very angry that she had been locked up. The stay in jail may have fueled her anger rather than have helped her see how bad things bring bad things. Maybe one day, all these things would add up and create a shocking awakening. This most recent walk on the wild side seemed to have only reaffirmed her belief that we were the meanest and worst parents ever.

A call came in at around eleven o'clock one night. As usual, it scared me a great deal. Wow, had I ever been conditioned. Thankfully, this time the call was from California. It was Megan's father calling to tell us she was threatening to drive her car off a cliff. He had also heard so many idle threats in the past, he like us, had to take her seriously because of the real attempts. Connie called her cell phone several times, but she didn't answer. We had no idea what was happening. Connie called as many family members as she could reach and asked them all to pray for Megan, and we all made that evening an evening of prayer.

Exhausted, with no word from Megan, we fell asleep. It was as if we had fallen asleep in God's arms. We fell asleep not knowing if morning would bring another discussion with Megan, an argument, or the need to make funeral arrangements. While the amount of sleep was minimal, we woke amazingly rested. I woke at five o'clock in the morning and went into the kitchen to make coffee. The sun coming through the skylight was warm on my neck as I stood by the coffee pot waiting for the first cup. The smell of the fresh coffee and the taste of the vanilla creamer brought a settling feeling. It was a rare peaceful start to a day. When Connie woke, we would begin our search for Megan, but now I was determined to enjoy the calm.

I turned and looked out the front window and saw Megan's car in the driveway. I went outside to check on her and found her inside, safe, and sound asleep. It was one of the greatest feelings of relief we had ever felt. God had heard all the prayers for Megan and had clearly been faithful by taking care of everything that night while we got some much-needed rest. We know it, but I wonder if she ever understood what He had done for her.

At nine o'clock that morning, Connie found someone who would work with Megan. Interestingly, this guy's name was Angel. She would need to drive twenty miles to meet with him at the health facility. Megan seemed depressed and tired but agreed to go. They got into Megan's car and off they went.

They spent hours with him talking and trying to figure out the best way to help Megan. He felt she was too attached to drugs and alcohol and needed to go to a rehab center before anything could change. He set up an appointment with the rehab center giving Connie and Megan enough time to drive across town.

The longer they drove, the more resistant Megan became. As time went on, the yelling and screaming started, and as time passed, it got extremely intense. It was clear she had no intention of going there. Connie was trying so hard to help this child get a life but was met with screaming and yelling every step of the way. Connie persisted and finally got Megan into the building to be assessed.

Megan met with a counselor but walked out of the meeting demanding the keys to her car. Connie refused, so Megan got on her cell and called the police. The arguing and fighting over the keys continued outside in front of a group of people while Megan continued demanding Connie give them to her.

The police arrived, discovered the car was in Megan's name, and made Connie give her the keys. Connie pleaded with the police, telling them she had recently threatened to drive off a cliff. They told her there was nothing they could do, it was her car. That was the kind of help we were used to getting from the people we expected help from. Over and over again, we seemed to be told, "Too bad people, you are out there all on your own."

Connie had no choice but to turn over the car keys, reminding Megan that car was nearly out of gas. Megan approached every person she could find begging for gas money. Unfortunately for her, most of the people standing nearby saw and heard the entire conflict and wouldn't help her. Filled with rage, she jumped into the car and drove off. Connie went back into the rehab center, found a quiet place, and sat down.

The entire time Megan was gone, Connie prayed that no one would give her gas money, and no one did. Another God answered prayer. It seems the only success we ever had in all of this, was when God answered prayers. Nothing we did in our own power ever worked. Nothing we did by going to others ever worked. Clearly, without Him helping us, she would be lost forever. Half an hour passed, and Megan returned, still out of gas, and agreed to go into rehab. She was evaluated and found to be needing a thirty-day stay. Attempting to help get her under control, they medicated her with some strong medicine. Her speech was slurred, and she exhibited very little energy or fight. It might remind you of a TV show where a bear got loose in a town, and they had to shoot it with a tranquilizer. She could move under her own power but had no desire to move far or fast, if at all. Seeing her like that just made Connie sick. I can't begin to imagine how many times Connie's heart had been broken by such dealings with Megan. Now nineteen years old, Megan continued to declare Connie to be the absolutely worst mom in the world. Megan had no idea how many tears her mom has cried, how many sleepless nights she had worried through, nor how many times her heart had been broken in all of this. No matter how awful Megan got, Connie didn't have it in her to turn away when her child was in need. Even though Megan was now legally an adult and was responsible for her own life, Connie never stopped trying and caring.

During these times, we learned there is a fine line between helping and enabling a person. Such a fine line only served to add more stress and concern to every decision we made. We were being buried under the negative things of our lives. The pile always got bigger, never smaller. It was heavy, consuming, suffocating, and painful. It felt like having a couple tons of warm manure dumped on you.

While Megan was being evaluated, something had to be done about her apartment. She would be with them for thirty days then off to a group home for a while. We talked to the landlord, advising them of her condition, and that she would be in a program and would not return. I got the keys from Megan, drove across town, and packed all her belongings in my truck. I then spent a couple hours cleaning the place.

Part of the terms of her release after the thirty days was that she lived in a halfway house. She would have chores, never one of her favorite things, group sessions and counseling. All of that was set up to help her look at life differently and to ease back into her life slowly.

A halfway house is one where the person could leave for work but had meetings and a curfew. The first one was a Christian home in which she lasted only a short time before getting kicked out for bad behavior. Off to another halfway house and was also kicked out of that one. Then off to a three-quarter house that offered greater freedom, yet she was kicked out of that one as well.

It seemed that easing her back into the world was not going to work, and she ended up living with us again. We should have put a revolving door in our house for as many times as she moved in and out. Each time I vowed it was the last time, but something deep inside will not let you give up on your kids. We kept believing one day something would click, and we would all have a normal life. We were her parents and had to do what had to be done, like it or not. Know this, moving her from apartment to apartment and in and out of our home was getting very old and exhausting. In spite of all the drama and failed hopes and dreams, we miraculously hadn't completely given up.

We got her home and settled her back into her old room. Seeing what the medication did to her broke our hearts. It all seemed so senseless and unnecessary. So many times she was normal, and then the next minute, she was replaced by her evil twin. Time passed, and even with the medication, the fighting escalated. Before we knew it, our life was miserable again. The first time I heard this remark, it was this way, "My dad told me you are not my real dad, and I don't have to listen to you!" After that I was continually told, "You're not my real dad!" Would somebody please tell me why I am still here?

I can't even imagine how many times we prayed that this time it would all work out. I can't tell you how many hours we spent wondering why it never did. Why couldn't she see the light and settle down? Why didn't she want to make her life a better place and have a better relationship with us? Sadly, I don't think even she had answers for those questions and neither did we. Assessments, evaluations, counselors, even medication didn't work. Why not?

She continued to demand we abide by her wishes, and all too often, when she couldn't make us do what she wanted, she threatened to kill herself. We were being held hostage and ineffective as parents by her threats.

We had tried everything we could think of. We tried everything the counselors suggested. We finally reached the point we were completely out of ideas. We had no idea what to do or how to handle her. She was out of control and refused to listen to reason from anyone.

One of the last therapists to see her assessed her and told us what we had been dealing with was nothing more than extremely bad behavior. He advised us to stop all medications, stop putting up with her nonsense, and to not allow her to live with us any longer. He felt the medication was just making matters worse.

She resisted any and all efforts to help her. Evil was rearing its ugly head in her words and actions. When we took her to church with us, she would sit and laugh hysterically. Anything religious made her worse. Seeing how she responded to everything and anything about God was like watching a movie about a person possessed by evil. It was scary to see, and it was scary to know that person was in your own home.

One Saturday, early in the afternoon, Megan, Connie, and I were in our bedroom, having what started out to be a regular discussion about Megan being given tighter restrictions as to how late and often she could go out. She had come home late the night before, and as we passed one another in front of the large living room windows, I could smell pot. Pot and alcohol were both on the list of "no can do" while living in our house. It was a list she agreed to in order to move back in with us. That breach in our agreement got her an earlier curfew and less times out until she could be trusted again.

Needless to say, at her age, we had no legal ability to restrict her or set any kind of rules at all. However, she had agreed to what we felt was fair or not live in our home, the choice was hers.

There was a party she had been planning to attend for a couple weeks, and now was not permitted to go. She was objecting to our decision, but we would not budge. Then she objected to having any rules to follow at all. Again, we didn't budge. She got more and more aggressive and pointed out she was old enough that she didn't have to listen to us. We agreed, but that also meant she would have to move out again. We heard the part about pot being okay with her father, again, and again, we didn't budge. She got angrier and angrier. She had every intent of attending this party, we didn't budge.

Anything that resembled a thought filled discussion had long passed, and now we were headed back into all too familiar territory. Here we were, Connie and I locked in intense verbal combat with Megan. This was not unfamiliar ground as the battling had at this point continued to escalate for thirteen years, beginning with bad behavior on our wedding day and being defiant about helping the family when we cleaned the house.

Connie and I patiently explained she had done this to herself. We explained we had a younger girl at home who we did not want exposed to such things. We explained that she was proven to have an addictive personality, and that we were trying to keep her from falling into an addictive pattern.

We would explain, and she would scream, shout, and argue. We explained more, and she screamed louder. As always, the screaming changed from the original topic to us being lousy, mean, and horrible parents. The older Megan got, the more punishing her choice of words had become. Her mother's heart had been torn apart over and over, and I could see in her eyes, this was developing into another one of those life-sucking, multi-hour episodes.

Connie and I sat united on our bed while Megan's defiant posture was portrayed from an overstuffed chair nearby. It was late afternoon, and the arguing and yelling had gone on for nearly two hours. Any interjections we made, trying to help Megan to understand our position, were bullied over by the increased volume of her ranting. We would respond to her ranting, and she would lash back for fifteen minutes with things that didn't even make sense. Eventually, we would get a word in, and then she would have the floor for the next twenty minutes. We had explained our position and why we did what we did in every way possible and were now drained, overpowered, and forced to sit and listen.

My head was killing me, and I was sick to my stomach. I wondered when I would reach the point where I would have no strength left for such battles. This was one of a hundred arguments we had had, and it was one of the worst. I was sick and exhausted as was Connie, but there was no end to the conflict in sight. She would not give up, she was relentless. Years of such fighting had taken a toll on us both, and it seemed our battles had gotten so crazy, we didn't even know this nineteen-year-old anymore. Scripture encourages us to hate the sin and not the sinner, but it was getting harder and harder to separate the two. I thought maybe if I did let myself hate this kid, I would feel better. I wanted to hate the one who was making our lives so miserable. I thought I could easily justify my hate because of what I had been put through for so long. The problem was, I don't think God would have seen any hate I let grow in me as justified. Try as I might to hate her, there was this "thing" deep inside me that would not let that happen. I continued to persevere against my flesh that wanted to hate. By the way, I now know the "thing" deep inside me was the small, sweet, encouraging voice of God. I was a child of His, and He was not going to let me hate this person, who was another one of His children, no matter what.

I needed something to hang on to, some hope to grasp at. We tried everything we could think of. We pleaded, held our ground, took her to counselors, psychologists, psychiatrists, and even to court before a judge. We argued; we didn't argue. We talked; we didn't talk. We tried to create a healthy relationship with Megan in every way we could, only to be rejected over and over. No matter what we did or tried, it was wrong. No matter what she did or didn't do, we were wrong. We lived a life filled with desperation and despair. Nothing ever got better.

Megan had a forceful approach. Coupled with her very big voice, she could overpower any contender with the sheer amount of words she used. She would rant without stopping and was so busy screaming that I doubt she ever heard anything we said. She would scream things we couldn't understand, and while we were trying to grasp what she meant, she would launch another attack. In such arguments, we were most always on the defensive just trying to keep up with her rantings. While she seemed to deeply enjoy a good fight, I didn't. I really wanted nothing to do with it. I wanted it out of my life.

I could stay and fight another fight, or I could plan my escape. What I would give for a normal life without this kid and without this constant fighting. I wanted to run, to pack up, and to get out of there. I would often tell myself, she was not my kid, I owed her nothing. If she wanted me gone, who could blame me for granting her such a wish? The answer to that question was I would blame me. I quit and ran from my two previous marriages, I couldn't do that again. What kind of man would I be if I left? I couldn't leave Connie to endure this war alone. I could not desert her during this mess. I am not being over dramatic here for I truly believed if it didn't stop, it could one day kill her or cause her to lose her mind. It is hard to put into words where we were at that time. Trying to explain our desperation, fatigue, and feelings would be like me trying to explain E=MC squared.

We were far beyond the limits of what we could deal with. Considerations to stay, fight, and help made sense, but in utter desperation, there was still that little voice, ever growing louder, urging me to save myself. That little voice kept telling me this kid was not my responsibility. Life could be so good, and it could happen with very little effort. In the time it would take me to pack a few things and call an attorney, I could be free of this forever and spare myself what would be many more years of this insanity. I could not understand why Megan wanted a life filled with such trouble and conflict. Why, oh why, could she not just want a normal life and work as hard toward that new life as she did toward chaos? It seemed like all it would take was a simple decision on her part and life could be good.

Her role as the victim continued to play well. She should have received an award for her portrayal of that character. In the heat of this battle, we again heard of poor Megan who was so mistreated and never got what she wanted. Her words, "I never get what I want," brought to mind another battle years ago when she expressed the same view. Every time I heard that, pictures of my growing up family life flashed through my mind. Why, oh why, couldn't I have that?

Never get what you want? What are you talking about? I thought. I saw dance lessons and recitals with expensive costumes. I saw great birthdays parties for her, Easter baskets and Valentine's Day gifts for her. I remembered the pile of gifts in front of her waiting to be opened every Christmas morning. I saw a closet full of nice clothes, a nice room of her own. I saw myself co-signing for a car for her and moving her place to place. I saw her going to one of the best school systems in the area. She had braces, and nice teeth as a result. I saw her every need cared for. I had no idea what she was talking about. She could go to sleep every night because we lived in a great and safe neighborhood. I could not understand how she felt she didn't have everything she needed.

That particular time, I had the wisdom to, again, ask her what exactly it was she wanted. She re-stated her greatest wish that she wanted me, and the daughter God had blessed Connie and me with, gone. Years had passed, and Megan continued to do what she could to make life to go back to where it was before me. She never stopped wanting to have her mom and older sister, Sarah, living together with her once again. She made her point loud and clear repeatedly, how I was not wanted nor was my only daughter. I thought, "After all it cost me and after all I had done and continued to do, you want me gone? How dare you! Well, I wanted me gone too! How do you like that smart guy?"

Megan wasn't holding anything back in this battle. She appeared to have used everything she could think of to inflict hurt and suffering. This was another one of those times we felt we were face-to-face with evil itself. Connie and I wrestled with thinking of Megan in such a way. We lost the real Megan somewhere along this horrible journey, and what was left was this, whoever she was.

I can't describe how deep into the pit of despair we had fallen. It was very dark, cold, and lonely in there. We had been down there so long we had a hard time even looking up to see if there was any light above. We almost didn't even care anymore. We began feeling like all we could do was sit there, take it, and not even fight back. We had all but given up. We prayed, day after day, that God would get us through that day. Sometimes we prayed that He would at least get us through that moment. Some of those days were the worst days ever, and others were the worst days ever times two. Happy days? You must be joking.

The battle raged on, and in her last attempt to force us to give her what she wanted, Megan threatened to kill herself. At this point, you could probably attach "again" to the end of every sentence I write. You certainly could attach "again" to the end of this suicide threat.

Here we are, beaten up after at least three hours of fighting. We were exhausted, throats dry, eyes burning, then finally confronted with "Fine, I will just kill myself." You might be thinking many kids threaten this to get what they want. I do agree, but remember, she had already overdosed twice. Her previous overdoses gave some validity to her threat.

Connie and I looked at each other, our eyes lacking any spark of hope. We had nothing left. Our brains were foggy, empty, and actually hurt. What were we supposed to do? We had no clue. I felt like a balloon with a slow three hour leak. There was a little air left in me that I was struggling to hold on to. In that moment, it felt like someone had come along with a razor blade, slashing my imagined balloon-like existence while the little air I had left gushed out. I was completely drained and could barely breathe. Connie sat there wordless and almost limp. Her very spirit and soul had to have been raw and drained of life.

This was her daughter. This was the little bright-eyed child who had at one time brought sparkle and laughter and joy into every room she entered. She had to be wondering what happened to the daughter who loved her mom so much. What happened to that fun, wonderful daughter who cuddled with her mom every chance she got and loved swimming in the Cajuzzi? I cannot even begin to understand what Connie must have been going through, yes, again. Maybe she wanted to run. Maybe she also wanted to have all of this out of her life.

It looked like she was completely spent. She couldn't cry anymore; her tears were gone. She didn't share how she felt because it seemed her ability to feel was also gone. She had become numb to life and numb to the awful world we lived in. Those changes that had taken my wife, were changes that had changed her forever. She was no longer the person I met so many years ago. Her daughter had forever changed her, and as I write this, I hope she will one day get back what had been taken from her in all of this. How could I help? How could I protect the wonderful wife God had given me? How could I stop this craziness? There was nothing I could do; I was helpless. All I could do was watch and listen and try to inject some sense into this fight, and that was not working at all.

After her suicide threat, Megan stopped talking. Thank God for small blessings, she finally shut up. She played her ace card and was patiently waiting for a response. I imagine, she thought she had beaten us, again. Megan had to be confident we knew she was willing to take pills again. She must have believed we would do anything to keep her from making another overdose attempt. Yes, she must have thought she had us locked in. Checkmate.

I sat lifeless for a moment, then stood and walked into our bedroom closet. Returning from the closet, I walked straight to Megan, stood before her calm and peaceful while pondering my next action. Deciding to go forward with my plan, I raised my hand holding a .32 caliber pistol. At eye level to Megan, I pulled back the slide, cocked the gun, and placed it on her lap. I stepped back to watch her reaction. My words to her were, "Okay, just do it already." She sat motionless, staring at the gun for what seemed like an hour. Again, I spoke, "Megan, just do it, or shut up about it. This is your chance, either do it, or never, ever bring it up again." She slowly sat back in the chair, resting her hands beside her. I gave her several more minutes to think things over before picking up the gun. My next words were a clear instruction that she was never, ever to threaten us like that again. Megan agreed. Conflict over. Threats over. Sigh. We prayed for sleep, a good sleep. A good sleep for all of us.

I wrestled a great deal with putting that event in print as I can imagine getting blasted by professionals and their opinions. My decision to share this was to be real and to express our complete and utter desperation along with the level of our constant conflict. I also wanted to be truthful even if it opened me up for criticism. A person not having lived through so many years of this has no idea of what it does to you and everyone in the home. I was desperate, out of ideas, and had gotten no help from professionals, or the law. I wanted to protect my wife and take at least one tool from Megan's war chest once and for all. We had tried everything but were still living in a pit where hope and faith no longer existed. Honestly, there had been a brief moment months earlier when I sat alone with my face in my hands, trying to imagine my future.

The picture of what most likely laid ahead brought nothing but anguish. In that moment, I thought of how that very same gun pointed at me could end this torture for me with a quick squeeze of the trigger. Thankfully, all be it birthed of desperation, it was a passing thought and not a real consideration.

Life as it was could not continue. Thankfully, and I am sure with God's help, those suicide threats stopped. Megan never again threatened to harm herself.

Sharing what I did with you is NOT in any way advice to you. It was a desperate act of a desperate person. We were a family in an ever-growing battle for the previous thirteen years. We were at the point we were reaching critical mass quickly. It had to stop before meltdown. I could not go on like this anymore. We could not go on like this anymore.

I hope the following information will ease your mind. While I was in the closet getting the gun, I removed the magazine and checked the chamber to make sure it was empty before setting it on her lap. She was never in any danger from the gun regardless of her decision. Interestingly, as I see it now, her decision revealed a great deal about where she was mentally. If she had picked up the gun and pulled the trigger, we would know how severe her needs were, and we would have taken suitable action.

While this particular battle was over, the war would rage on well past these thirteen years for an additional fourteen years. That time frame encompasses the entire length of our marriage at the writing of this story thus far.

So, here I am, sharing "one" of the most extreme events of our struggle. Take note that at this time, we were only near midpoint in our marriage. The battles escalated, and we experienced things we could never have imagined, nor do I have the energy to put them all on paper. We will have to endure so much more. Times were coming that would make me wonder if I was the one who had lost his mind.

One thing I did learn in this is that I married her mom, and whether or not she was my kid, I was responsible for her - no matter what. I was responsible to care for her, protect her, and keep her safe - no matter what.

How did our plans for a happy home and family get shattered? How did so much seem to have gone so wrong? Did God ever hear our prayers and pleading? Why had He left us alone in all of this? Could I hold on to my faith? Had I given up on God? Had God given up on me? Why was this happening? We had no answers, only lots and lots of questions.

I wondered why she hated me so much. I wondered if I could stick it out. I wondered if I even wanted to stick it out. I wondered if the love I felt for her could eventually turn to hate. I wondered if I was being punished for being married and divorced those two times. I could not understand how I had gotten myself in such a mess, nor could I figure out how to get out of it.

I was riding out of control on a train at full speed with the engineer missing and the bridge out ahead. It seemed the best I could hope for was to survive the crash. But could I survive?

CHAPTER 11

Drug Dealers, Morocco, Enough

A few days after that horrendous episode, things settled down some. Megan got inspired and found another new apartment, number five. With that, I loaded her up and moved her into her new place. Okay, I will not say again, again. Before long she got a job at a gas station a few blocks away. For what seemed like the hundredth time, things were calm and quiet. Then we got the dreaded call.

She was in jail again. A customer at the gas station left their credit card on the counter after paying for gas. Megan, a big believer in finders' keepers, decided to do a little shopping and charged a couple hundred dollars on this person's card. That little crime spree put her back in jail for another ten days.

As I have said several times, she is a great agitator and manipulator. Those negative attributes drove the police at this station absolutely crazy. Within a few days, they called us, begging us to bring her a TV or something to shut her up. It was against the jail rules to have a TV in the cell, but they couldn't take it anymore. Stop here for a minute. Think hard about what I just shared. She was in a police station. With police officers all around her. They were there with badges, guns, and more authority than most people around us. Yet, she was driving them mad. They could not control her at all. That is really saying something. We understood what they were dealing with and brought an old spare TV to the station. Sometimes little things such as this seem to validate how you felt. I kept thinking, officer, you have no idea but thanks for helping me feel I have not been overreacting.

Here is an interesting thought. Remember how, near the start of our story, I wrote about the fact that everyone loved Megan and how her behavior away from home led them to believe we were the problem? At this point that scenario has changed, and it has been years that anyone having contact with Megan could not wait to get rid of her. There was no longer anyone in her corner defending her actions because her actions were horrible. Her behaviors caused most people to not want to deal with her in any way. Eventually, I guess the truth does come forward no matter how subtly.

After being released and back in her apartment, she reconnected with the crowd from Morocco. Going to jail hurt her financially, making her desperate for cash. This group of Moroccans told her they had a friend back home in Morocco who wanted to come to America. I can't remember the amount, but they said he would pay her, something like $5000, if she went to Morocco, married him, and brought him back here. They also advised her she would only have to stay married for one year to make it legal. After that, she could get a divorce and could go back to being single.

She stopped by our house one afternoon to share this newest plan. We had a lengthy discussion on the back deck about what marriage was all about, and that God surely would not honor such a thing. When she first got to the house, she was sure this was the way to go to solve her problems. Thankfully, when she left, she was unsure of what to do.

Days later, she advised us of her decision. She wanted an adventure and would go to Morocco to visit this guy and not get married.... unless, of course, it felt right. The hatching of Plan A followed.

She sold as much of her apartment furnishings as she could. I picked up the rest in my truck and loaded our garage with the leftovers, again. This time the stack of her life's possessions was smaller than it had been in the past. The big sale afforded her enough money to make the trip and off she went. Everyone was completely against it. Everyone tried to convince her she was making a mistake, but once again, she did what she wanted against all advice. And off she went, halfway around the world.

After a very short time in Morocco, Megan phoned telling us she was in love and would be getting married. She was married in the traditional Moroccan style. She was dressed in a very decorated white kaftan or wedding garment. She wore much traditional jewelry, and her eyes were darkened with kohl. Her feet and hands were painted in intricate geometrical designs by an artist using henna. Such designs are meant to ward off evil spirits and bring good luck. You may be thinking what I am thinking, "If only that would work." I can easily imagine she felt like a princess, something I can say with confidence she always wanted to be. We could only pray good things would come her way. The pictures she sent us via email drove home the fact that she was now in a different world. A world of which we had no understanding.

Maybe, just maybe, she had finally found happiness, someone to love and be loved by. Would she live out her life in Morocco with a new family? Had her dreams finally come true? We truly hoped so. Whether it made sense to us or not, we wanted her to have a life filled with all the love and good things we all want. I was not sad she was so far away because once again, we were outside of her reach and were being left alone.

Megan was happy and excited following the wedding. Morocco appeared to be giving her the life she had been searching for. As time passed, her phone calls expressed a certain sadness. I think she was becoming increasingly more homesick as days went by. Living in a very poor area and having no source of income afforded them nothing to do. Days would pass with sitting around the home and taking a walk here and there. For Megan, being homesick was one thing, add being bored with no excitement on the horizon, and that was something that would be close to unbearable for her.

Contemplating what life in America would be for them, she developed Plan B. The plan was to make their home here in the U.S. and eventually support his family in Morocco by sending them money. It was an honorable plan, and it made sense, not to mention it was what her husband wanted to do to begin with.

Her plan was to come back and work with immigration to get him moved here. If I remember correctly, her father bought her a ticket, you guessed it, back to Ohio.

Megan's father was successful, and as I mentioned, our finances were very up and down, mostly down. At this particular time, we were struggling again. While he was in a position to easily buy an airline ticket and send Megan anywhere he wanted, we were in no position to return the favor.

It would soon become a trend. Things would go bad for Megan, and he would send her to Ohio. He didn't want to deal with her, and she would end up back in Ohio. Like it or not, there was nothing we could do to stop or change that. It wouldn't take too many such, "here she comes" trips for me to lose my cool.

Again in Ohio, she found yet another place to live, that being number six, got a job, and began researching what needed to be done to get him here.

United States Immigration explained she was not making enough money to bring him here even though he was her husband. She would have to show significantly more financial stability before that could happen. There was one way around that impassible obstacle, but that would require the help of others. Megan began soliciting us and her father to sponsor him. What that entailed was us accepting financial responsibility for him, and Megan to guarantee his and her needs would be met. Apparently getting a job or two to do it on her own hadn't crossed her mind.

That was absolutely out of the question for any of us. If her lifestyle and track record had been more reliable, we might have agreed. If we had learned anything, we learned that Megan could take such a commitment and abuse it. If we had learned anything, we learned we would surely come out on the short end of the stick on this deal. I could imagine one day being hauled into court by the immigration department in response to a charge filed by Megan that we hadn't been taking care of them as we should. No way would I ever put myself in such a vulnerable position.

Attaching our finances to her life could easily ruin us if things went badly. That was a gamble larger than any of us were willing to take. We still had our youngest daughter at home and had to attend to her needs. We barely had enough income to support our regular living expenses, let alone to take on the risk of committing to immigration requirements.

Her plan to move her husband here now looked impossible. Of course, who was at fault for that? We were. In her eyes, it was another very good reason to take her rage out on us. The nasty, ugly attacks began. She relentlessly scolded us with the importance of getting her husband here, so they could make a new life. We never denied the validity of her plan, agreeing it would be a wonderful thing. But because of our limited income and the risk of being legally attached to her, this was something we couldn't and wouldn't do. It seemed she had no concern for us and what we were risking. She only cared about getting what she wanted, as usual.

Because we would not bend to meet her demands and attacks, we were once again the enemy, which brought all the same old exhibitions of resentment and anger into our lives. She seemed to lose her mind when things didn't go as planned. She couldn't think things through and had no ability to rationalize what was going on. She would not accept having her plans fail. In her mind it was unacceptable, and somehow, she would force them to happen.

In the process of her attempts to force life to go the way she wanted, all of us around her became victims of her fury. This was nothing new, we had seen it too many times and were ever so tired of dealing with it.

Plan A was to move to Morocco and have a life. Plan B was to move her husband here and create a new life. We now moved on to Plan C, which was to move back to Morocco. She executed Plan C, but it wasn't long before she and her husband started fighting.

Moving to a new country had not changed her response to life's ebb and flow. In Morocco, the entire family lived in the same house, and everyone knew everyone's business. Fighting was one thing that could never be kept secret. Now it seemed she had a group of people in Ohio who were unfair to her, another group in California, and now Morocco held a new group of people who just did not understand her. How can so many people in so many places be the source of her life's troubles while she did everything right?

This was the pattern we witnessed so many times. It was similar to the *Starship Enterprise* getting too close to a black hole and getting sucked in. When life got bad according to Megan's definition, those close to her got drawn in as well. Megan called often telling us how much they hated her. She was hurt, felt rejected and disillusioned. She could not take it any longer and had to move back to the United States. We felt sorry for her and were sorry her dreams had not come true. Honestly, I may have been saddest of all. I am embarrassed to say, I hoped she would have found a new life in Morocco, so we could enjoy normal lives here.

Now Plan D. I am making this short, she came back. We were told that her father had bought her another plane ticket to Ohio. Here we were, again, Mr. and Mrs. pick up the pieces.

I resented and was angered by the fact that whenever Megan and her father deemed a move was necessary, her coming to Ohio was shoved down our throats. Our life was put into chaos regardless of what we might be doing. We had to drop everything, pick her up, and get her settled while dealing with all the drama. The hardest part of it was we never seemed to have a choice, we were never asked, we were simply advised of what we had to do. This was reminiscent of living in California when the kids were little. The girls would plan to spend a weekend with their father, but we had to remain on call. Plans almost never went as we were told, and we had to always be nearby to take the kids back. This was all getting to be too ridiculous.

We hoped her recent experiences in Morocco brought changes in how Megan viewed life. While we continued to hope, we also prepared for the battles that would most likely come our way. The thought of living in the midst of battles and fighting again, made me sick.

This is one of those spots that is unclear. I can't remember how Megan ended up on the streets again, but she did. I must give her some credit here. This time she didn't ask to come and live with us. This time she seemed to be trying to do it on her own. We received several calls during her time of homelessness, expressing her fear of being followed or asking for gas money. She eventually moved in with some guys who were dealing drugs downtown. She was desperate for a warm place to sleep but had no idea how this perceived kindness would turn her room into a prison. According to Megan, those people would not let her leave the apartment unescorted. They would not let her make phone calls unless they were there to hear who she was talking to and what she was saying.

If I remember correctly, they made her keep her phone locked in her car, and they held onto her keys. That way, someone would walk her to the car, let her make a call, lock the phone back up, and walk her back to the apartment. She was under a watchful eye all day, every day.

She could only take feeling like a captive for so long and was starting to break down. These guys had a big business to protect and controlling what she did prevented Megan from leaking any information about their activities. She felt trapped and imprisoned, needing to get away. A prospect that was easier said than done.

Somehow, Megan snuck out, broke the window of her car, got her phone, and called Lizzie. Megan planned a meeting place with Lizzie and hid until she arrived. Unknown to us, Lizzie and a friend left a young women's renewal meeting at church and headed downtown to meet her. Here again, did Megan give any thought to Lizzie's safety? Did her thoughts ever involve the wellbeing of anyone else? It would seem not. Why would she bring her little sister into a potentially dangerous situation like that? On the other hand, she was desperate, and I guess we can't blame her for that.

When they arrived, they found Megan hiding near her car. The drug dealers were nowhere in sight. The girls grabbed what they could from the car and sped off, leaving Megan's car behind.

Megan was mentally out of it again and needed help. Lizzie didn't know if it was fear, drugs, or alcohol that was making her act so strange. She decided the best thing to do was to call Connie and tell her Megan seemed to be out of her mind. Connie called friends in the medical field, trying to find a place that could help Megan. She was referred to a rehab center in the country.

Desperate to help her sister, Lizzie and her friend began the hour and a half drive to get her to the facility, so she could be examined and receive help. Megan was furious and was determined to escape. They were in the middle of nowhere when, at the first opportunity, Megan jumped out of the car and ran off. It was winter, twenty degrees outside, and all she had with her was what she was wearing and her cell phone. Her attire did not include a coat.

Lizzie was worried about Megan freezing but couldn't find her. After an hour of driving around, she gave up and came home. Lizzie's efforts to rescue Megan and get her help were met with an ungrateful attitude and refusal to be helped. She was hurt by Megan's behavior and her running away from the help she clearly needed. Lizzie was crushed to the point of giving up hope that anyone could ever help her sister. To tie up a loose end, we had Megan's car towed to our house late one night to avoid another confrontation with the drug dealers. We still have no idea what Megan did that night.

Megan hung out with her husband's friends for a few days, trying to figure out what to do. While there, she found out that her husband was very sick. The start of Plan E.

She raised some cash and flew to Morocco to help. No one at his house was doing anything for him. Most likely because of having no money rather than a lack of caring. She loved him and had to do everything she could to help. He lost a great amount of weight, was extremely weak, and was coughing up blood. Luckily, she brought all the money she had with her because it took three visits to the clinic to figure out what was wrong.

He had tuberculosis and was really in trouble to the degree that he might not live. She got him the medications he needed and nursed him back to some of his former self.

I say this confidently; I believe Megan saved his life. In the middle of a life of craziness and unrest, God used this lost and confused girl. He sent her to rescue a man, her husband, in a little poor neighborhood in a strange country.

Megan exhibited Christ on Earth to this man and his family. In this case, she was Christ's hands and feet, giving all she had in the world to save him. We have never doubted the great, loving heart she had as a child, we simply couldn't understand how it got completely buried. Every chance she got, she let him know that Jesus saved his life. She even got him an Arabic Bible. She may have been there to save his life, but now his soul was what concerned her.

We were all very proud of her for doing what she did. We still are. Megan also risked her own health in the process. She had asthma most of her life, making her lungs weaker than normal. We were concerned that she might be highly susceptible to the tuberculosis.

This was the girl we knew was deep inside. She had always exhibited a caring for others, just not us. I wondered why this wasn't the part of who she was that she would want to grow more into. It seemed simple that a choice to spend her life caring for other people could dramatically alter her life's course. We believe she could have been, and maybe still could be, a wonderful nurse.

Hear this as well, no matter how awful a person may seem, God sees value in them. God clearly used Megan to save this man's life, and the only person who could accomplish that was this mixed-up, lost girl. I believe the lesson is that if God never gives up on people and sees value in them, then perhaps we should look at others the same way.

Megan's husband had been on his medication for around two months and feeling better. Yet again, there was trouble and turmoil. Again, we got a call telling us her father was buying tickets for her to come back to Ohio. Onto Plan F.

Connie met Megan at the airport, and fearing for her health, she immediately took her to a clinic to be tested for tuberculosis. She drove with the car windows open, hoping to keep the car full of fresh air and maybe lessen the possibility of the disease getting to her. Megan tested fine, and she, again, moved in with us. Another miracle in her life. We saw it that way and hoped she would understand God was watching over her and protecting her from disease.

To shorten this up some, there were problems and fighting again, so she moved back to Morocco, Plan G. This trip met with the same unhappy results, and she planned another trip back to the United States. Plan H.

Isn't this hard to imagine? These trips were not years apart but short periods of time. I get worn out writing about them. I cannot imagine how anyone lived them. I believe she never stayed in Morocco for more than a few months. Can you imagine setting her up in a place and moving her out time after time? Can you imagine the cost to her father who bought most of the tickets? There can be no doubt that all of us tried so hard to help her find her way. Doing all that wouldn't be so bad, except for the fact she never really seemed to acknowledge how much everyone was doing for her. Instead, when something didn't go right, we were all blasted for being horrible people.

Life never had time to be normal for any of us. While she was gone, we might enjoy a couple months before the phone calls started. Then she would come back, and only a month or so would go by before the fighting started, and then she would leave again. Back and forth, time after time. To say it was exhausting is an understatement.

Before we knew it, another phone call from Megan telling us of Plan H. Her father had bought her another ticket back to Ohio. This one may have driven me into fight or flight mode. I was again done. I could not take it. I was tired of those two dictating our lives and upsetting any chance of us living life the way we wanted to. We could never get into any type of rhythm, we could never make our plans work. It seemed we were the trash heap where failed plans were dumped. We were the cleanup team, the safety blanket, the servants who did their bidding. After all these years and after all those moves, apartment to apartment and country to country, I declared an end to our participation.

I emailed her father, refusing to pick her up, refusing to find her a place to stay, and refusing to help in any way. In short, I declared if she came back here, he would have to do everything from picking her up to getting her settled himself. I would not do it again. Plan H was aborted, and thanks be to God, she went to California and moved in with her dad, Plan I. She has settled in California and has never again moved to Morocco nor Ohio.

Before long, the fighting began. We lived in California for many years, and I smiled every day. Even when life was hard, I smiled. How could anyone be crabby with all the opportunities, the sun, warm temperatures, sea, sand, and all the beauty? How in the world could the wonder of the west coast not make difficulties not so difficult? How could living in such a climate not motivate you to want to live the best life you could?

Sadly, Megan exhibited the ability to be angry anywhere and everywhere. Truthfully, I don't think she was angry about being there, she was simply angry she didn't go where she wanted to go, Ohio. She continued to express her anger through what I imagined her motto might be, "I can't get what I want, so I will take it out on you." While living in California, Megan made sure her father and his wife got their share of bad attitude as well.

Her anger toward us reached another all-time high, and she had no problem telling us how much she hated us. This time was worse than ever before, by far. Her father let her read the email I sent about us not taking responsibility for having her come back to Ohio. To make a bad relationship even worse, she took the email personally, feeling I had rejected her and rage once again reared its ugly head. She called our youngest, telling her how horrible a dad I was and how her father was what a real dad should be like. She called us continually and yelled and screamed at her mother, telling her what a horrible mom she was and that she hated her. If she called Connie and she didn't answer, the next time they did talk, she would scream at her and accuse her of ignoring her and demand to know why she had not answered the phone. Can you imagine? Megan exhibited zero respect for me, which is almost understandable, but to have no respect for her mom, that was beyond unacceptable.

Connie got to the point that she, too, would jump every time the phone rang and became afraid to answer it but also afraid not to answer it. Megan continually called and yelled at me over the phone about how mean I was and that I ruined her life. Every bad thing in her life was my fault. If I had not been such a horrible person, she would never have done any of the things she had done. In a way, I was handling all she could throw at me, but Connie was beaten down farther and farther. It was horrible to watch, and nothing I did could change what was happening.

I continued feeling bad for Connie. She gave so much to help Megan, even losing a job trying to help. None of that mattered because according to Megan, she was the worst mother on Earth. Being told these things over and over again for so long had to have changed Connie's view of herself as a mom. When you hear such things over and over, you cannot help but wonder if they are true. I think Connie began to believe, just maybe, she was the world's worst mom. Even now, some of her joy of life has been taken because of all of this, but I am hoping one day she will find it again.

Again, I began to feel guilty, that perhaps, if I had left earlier or if I had never come into the picture, or maybe, just maybe, if I left now, something could be salvaged for this family. I felt I had indeed ruined everyone's life.

It was at this time we were preparing to move out of Ohio and were hopeful once we did, things would somehow get better. The calls were relentless and growing in the level of meanness. It got so mean and full of evil that Megan called her mom, telling her she was coming to Ohio, planned to tie us up, and make her watch while she killed me and then would kill her. Megan told her she would never know when she was coming, but she was planning it right now. We didn't take it seriously, but the words and the hatred behind them did almost as much damage as if we would have believed she had the ability to carry out such threats.

She began to tell a new story that she, conveniently, just remembered.

127

She said it was so horrible she blocked it out all these years. The story went, when they were little, she, her older sister, and I were in my truck, taking a friend of mine home. The story was that my friend molested Megan while I did nothing about it. Interestingly, I do remember a comment she made to me after we drove my friend home that day. I was driving, Sarah sat in the middle, and Megan sat on my friend's lap. When we got home, she told me she could feel his penis when she was sitting on his lap. I was surprised she noticed and was uncomfortable but didn't think that much more about it other than sharing it with Connie. After some time passed, Megan's story became that my friend molested her while I molested her sister. Then the story eventually grew into one that had me molesting Megan.

The story always got worse and was never the same. There were never any details, just the basic story. She began calling the entire family, telling them I had molested her.

As I have said, she is relentless and can be convincing. How was I supposed to deal with that? I felt bad and hurt but didn't get angry. Maybe because I knew she wasn't telling the truth, and I trusted everyone would know that. Apparently, I was wrong.

The feeling that some family members may have been starting to doubt my innocence angered me but hurt more than anything. I could not be sure that what I was feeling was correct for little was said other than an odd comment here and there. It was one of those gut feelings a person gets when something is just wrong.

Me, the guy who loved kids, whose lifelong dream was to have a family? The guy whose kids' friends called dad. How could anyone ever doubt me? Our youngest defended me and joined the battle to protect my integrity and the truth. It got ugly.

I was crushed and lived in disbelief. I thought life had been awful and would continue to be awful. In a way, I began to accept that. I never expected life to go this way. This was something I was not prepared for. Just when I thought life could not get worse, it surely did.

I was haunted by thoughts of how much I gave to that kid. I was always there to bail her out, move her, go to court with her, kick guys out of her apartment, or sit and try to give sound advice. I never rejected her. I tried so hard to make her feel like part of a family from our wedding day on. Now at this point, I just needed to have her out of my life, and the only way it seemed I could do that was to get out of hers. Once, and for all.

Leaving was again the only thing that made sense. Leaving seemed to be the only hope for me to have a happy life. Leaving seemed like it might be the only thing that would give Connie peace. I tried everything. Everything failed. I was burned out.

The problem was I still couldn't make myself do it. Isn't it starting to sound like I had lost it? To some degree, I may have. How could I have kept coming to the same conclusion but continually do the opposite thing? No matter what I wanted for me, I couldn't leave Connie and Lizzie and Sarah. Sarah was now married and lived a couple hours away. I loved her and thought she might still need me around once in a while. It was fortunate at this point that she lived a couple hours away and was not in the middle of all this mess. That was an enormous blessing.

No matter how many times I felt I was done. No matter how many times I felt I had to save myself, somehow, I continued. It had to be the grace of God because my strength was long gone.

Talk about returning good with bad, I could write a new definition for that. She continued harassing the entire family until some of Connie's family began to see the truth. They, too, reached the point they were tired of the drama and refused to talk to her about such things.

While in California, with her mom's help, Megan saw some doctors who prescribed some medication for her. This time, it worked very well. The medication helped her to have dreams and goals and want to do things better. She spent a lot of time praying and studying the Bible, both morning and evening. It seemed she had again connected with God. It also seemed when she was in control, she knew exactly what to do.

She went to cosmetology school and got her hairdresser's license. Hooray! That was a very good thing she did for herself. She got an apartment and proudly began a life. Life got better and better. We were all amazed and wondered why it had taken so long to find such an easy solution.

Her harassing calls stopped. Maybe this time, it was really over. She was planning her future and was proud of herself. I was positive with all these good things happening, this time she would learn to accept success and enjoy life. Sadly, for her, it didn't work out quite that way.

She started taking more of her medication by two and three times the prescribed dosage. Why in the world would she do that? I have no idea. Sometimes I think she got bored or lonely or a little of both. Things had been coming together, I couldn't understand why she would make that kind of decision. One would think taking pills would be the action of someone on a downward spiral or one with no hope. She had experienced both of those scenarios, and I would think she would want to avoid any possibility of returning to them. I would never expect someone whose life is looking up for the first time in a very long time to do that, but she did. In her own experience, she knew the difference between things going well and desperation. You would think the years of living both ways would help her never want to return to the horrible way she had lived in the past.

She also began drinking again and that, combined with the medicine, just knocked her right out of reality. She began reading and interpreting the Bible. She had audible discussions with God and declared he was telling her the truth about how I had abused her and molested her. I remember her telling me that when I died, God would show me the truth.

She supposedly gained an amazing amount of wisdom right from God and was now a prophet. She could meet someone and instantly know that they had either been abused or molested. God was showing her these truths so she could help others. No one could tell her she was wrong about anything. She was the only one who had the truth. She was God's right-hand person here on earth.

Her relationship with her father was up and down. She felt she had the right to dictate how those around her should treat her, then judge them when they didn't live up to her dictates. I guessed she was treating him that way because we received our share of calls telling us he was not being a good father. She also managed to continue to express her hate for Connie and me because we didn't buy into all her stories. It seems having built a promising future she couldn't help but destroy it. Enter Plan J.

Against everyone's advice, she dumped it all and moved back to Morocco. It seems she had a self-destruction mode or fear of success that wrecked her life over and over.

The plan this time was to take her husband and move to a big city and become a hairdresser for tourists. While they researched the plan, she did some hairdressing locally, but they never made the move to the big city. About now, things are a little fuzzy, can you blame me? However, I am fairly sure there was a Plan K taking her back to California and a Plan L taking her to Morocco.

Home again in Morocco, life became another complete disaster. She talked of her husband being out of control and how the family hated her. She called the States in fear for her life. They were all after her, and she was afraid they were going to kill her this time. She was sure of it.

To top it all off, she had the feeling she was pregnant. If the family there found out she was pregnant, she would possibly never get out of the country. She pleaded for help before it was too late.

Another big, family time of prayer for Megan. We felt the only way she was going to get out of this mess was by the hand of God. She needed His help, and He was not stingy. Again, family all over the country prayed.

Plan M unfolded. She snuck out of the house one night and ran to the safety in the U.S. Consulate. She waited in the consulate, hoping for help getting out of the country. Connie's brother, who worked for an airline, got her an immediate emergency ticket back to California. He had sent it directly to the consulate. The consulate got her to the airport, and she was safely on her way back to California. If only she had signed up for frequent flyer miles, she could own a boat by now.

Now we find Megan back in California, possibly pregnant and living with her dad as they planned for her future. This last trip had scared her, something that didn't happen easily. The stories continued about how mean they were to her and how they threatened her. The entire family was thrilled she was back safe and hoped that her days of world travel would now be over.

As time passed, Megan began to admit that all the issues in Morocco were her fault. She had agitated them and made everyone angry. It was because of her behavior that they were all so mad at her. She also said her life was never in danger, she made it all up. That was one part of the story that was easy for us to believe.

Let me give you an idea of how difficult it was to deal with her stories. It is quite possible she might have originally told the truth, but now she confessed lying about no one wanting to hurt her. Hearing such changes in her "truth" you couldn't help but think she would spin a tale saying it was all her fault, so if she wanted to go back to Morocco, no one could tell her it was too dangerous. She could easily lay out plans like that covering all the details and no one would be the wiser. We may never really know the truth.

Of course, we all believed that she had been running for her life because as always, she was so convincing. I saw how upset Connie was and how the phone kept ringing with calls from family members worried about Megan.

All of that caring, all of that worrying, all because of a lie. Isn't that a bit cruel? I don't think any parent wants to believe their child is lying and trusts there is at least some truth in what they say. In this case, there was very little truth to her story. It was simply concocted to ensure she would get what she wanted, another trip back home. Truth or not, it is our responsibility to care for those we love. Connie worked so hard at helping Megan over and over and in the midst of all the crazy stuff. I never heard Connie complain or ever threaten to give up, it is just what we do as parents. Is it fair? Truthfully no. We come to realize we signed up for this, and no matter how tough or how ridiculous things get, we have to hang in there.

The dramatic issue in front of us for now was finding out the results of the pregnancy test. Megan never exhibited any real maturity and with all her other issues we wondered, "How could she care for a baby if the test came back positive?"

CHAPTER 12

Too Much

As time went by, more of the truth regarding the events in Morocco came out. Not surprisingly, the truth was quite different from the story we were told coercing us to get her back to the United States.

Megan and her father immediately began the search for her own place. In the midst of making her own residence become a reality, the pregnancy tests came back positive, and with that, many demands were issued to all of us.

Megan set about telling everyone what their responsibilities regarding her needed to be. Not once was there a "Please would you?" or anything resembling a request. We were living in South Carolina at the time, and she expected Connie to quit her job, leave me, and go to California to help her with her pregnancy. Connie's responsibility would continue to include being there when the baby was born and to take care of them for the first six months. This might sound humorous to you, as if I might be joking. I assure you, Megan was serious.

Connie made it clear that there was absolutely no way that was going to happen. As usual, that response infuriated Megan.

Failing to convince Connie using guilt tactics, she came up with another twist. She reminded Connie my dad died at sixty-two and told her she was hoping that as I neared the same age, I would be dead soon. This would then set Connie free to move to California to take care of her. Wouldn't you think after all these years, Megan would have given up the hope that she and her mom would one day be alone and living together? I told you she was stubborn and determined, but I think this sets some sort of record.

Suddenly, because of her pregnancy, she decided everyone close to her was there to care for her. It was all about her with absolutely no regard for anyone else's life. It was never as if any issue got resolved and it was gone. The repetition of attitudes, thinking, and actions eroded any hope we had for a normal life for any of us. This had been going on for so long it hurt us as much to watch her continually struggle as her attitude toward us hurt.

If you have issues, deal with them and then move on, at least you have some sense of progress. Years went by and she beat us up with the same thinking and issues, repeatedly. It was almost psychological warfare or a relentless cry for help. Who would ever know? In any event, we fought through it unharmed ... I think.

Megan's father saw no reason why she couldn't work to support herself until the baby was delivered. Megan complied and did some hair styling until the baby was born.

It's a girl! The delivery was normal, and the baby was beautiful and healthy. The whole family relaxed and celebrated with her. We had some concerns for the baby during the pregnancy because of all the alcohol, drugs, and medications she had used, but thank God, none of that affected the baby's health.

Megan spent a great deal of time on the phone with Connie, asking questions and getting guidance. The number of books she read about having the baby outdid the total number of books she read all through high school. Everyone sent gifts for the baby and congratulated her, expressing their best wishes.

Giving birth seemed to change her a great deal. She was calm, caring, and not the least bit aggressive or angry. We were amazed and happy, hoping once again, fingers crossed, life had come together for Megan. Again, just maybe our prayers had finally, and completely been answered.

She loved her little girl so much and was determined to be the best mom she could be. Her life had purpose and meaning, and to all of us, it was a wonderful turn around.

I can't remember if it was before the baby was born or after, but she divorced her husband who was still in Morocco. Making that decision was not easy for her. I am not sure how she felt about it because she has never shared her feelings with me. I can only imagine she had to deal with the death of another dream. Just like all of us, she probably wanted to be loved and may have thought she found the love she had been searching for only to have to give it up. That would not be an easy thing for any of us. It had not been an easy thing for me.

Something that struck us as amazing was it felt like the entire family had come together in support of Megan. Our family was functioning as a family should. It was something I thought we might never see. In all of this, we learned family is always there to pray with you when things are at their worst and celebrate with you when good things happen. As much as any of us may have ever felt isolated, the truth was we weren't.

Easter was getting close, and Megan planned a trip to Ohio to see her sister Sarah. Connie wanted to see both the girls and all the grand-babies, now numbering four. Connie was looking forward to enjoying the short homecoming of her daughter who had seemed to have continued to be her old self since giving birth.

We made plans to drive up from South Carolina to stay at my sister's house while she was away. From there, we planned to make the two-hour drive to Sarah's on the Thursday before Easter. We were going to spend that night and Good Friday there then drive back Friday evening. Megan was coming back to my sister's with us to spend a couple days before flying home to California.

I told Connie that I could not make myself go to Sarah's for Easter. After all that I had been through with Megan, I had no interest in seeing her, partly because of all the abuse stories she had told the family. I was also afraid my presence would cause another battle. I wasn't willing to take a chance that might ruin Easter for everyone.

During a phone conversation, Megan asked Connie if I was coming, to which she answered I was not. Megan asked why. Connie explained my reasons, and Megan completely understood.

Connie later told me that Megan cried. In all these past years, that was the first time I can think of that she cried. Megan further commented that she thought everyone knew she had been lying about me. She was literally shocked that anyone had given any credibility to what she had been saying. After that call, she phoned everyone in the family, telling them she lied and confessed I never beat her or molested her.

Megan hurt me a great deal, and in my humanness, I still wanted to hate her. She robbed me of a large portion of my life and happiness. She robbed much of the family of a normal life as well. Still, God graciously never let my anger and hurt turn into real hate. I didn't particularly like her nor have any desire to be around her, but I continued to wish the best for her. I think most of what I felt was a deep distrust for her. Connie told me what efforts Megan made to get me to come. Against my better judgement, I agreed to go but was still cautious.

It was a good time in spite of the fact I felt I was under a microscope the entire visit. Megan and I were semi-friendly, and I think we were both being cautious. I knew the kind of person she was, and if I played with Sarah's kids more than her baby, she would resent it, and I would be accused of liking them more, giving fuel to start another fight.

The entire day I made sure I was dividing my time equally. In the past, Megan would listen very closely and wait for one word she could take wrong, giving her justification to attack. Having lived with that for so many years, I watched every action and said very little all day. As time went on, I think we all relaxed a little and finally seemed to get past all the junk.

The ride home was almost a two-hour drive, and it went well. Connie had a VW convertible that Megan was dying to drive, so Connie let her drive. Megan was happy and excited and seemingly began to be the old Megan. I drove back with Lizzie.

I was amazed at how she had changed. Having this baby truly helped her become a calm and peaceful person, and it was great. This wasn't the first time I dared to believe all the craziness was finally over. Hey, one can hope, so let's give it another try.

We got back to my sister's, and I was exhausted. All the stress of being on my best behavior took its toll. I was also frustrated with having to continue being careful of everything I did and said for a couple more days and a little frustrated with Connie for putting me through all this. I laid down on the big leather couch in the family room and tried to take a nap. It was so quiet and peaceful, and what a healing break from all the high energy of the grandkids who always have more energy than me.

Connie, Megan, and the baby went upstairs to unpack. They were up there for a long time when Connie came down and started asking me what I was angry about. I told her I was just tired, admitted I was a bit cranky, and wanted to take a nap. I was cranky, I was tired, but I was also tired of watching my every word and action. She could not accept that answer, she kept at me wanting an explanation. After explaining a couple times, I shouted at her to leave me alone. Now I was angry for real. Connie and Megan must have been sitting upstairs judging my actions just as I had feared. I had lived under this same scrutiny in this family for half my life, and here we go again. I was so sick of it.

Ten minutes passed when Connie, Megan, and the baby came down all packed up. I asked Connie where they were going, to which she replied, "Back to Sarah's!"

Megan said she did not need to have her baby around negative energy. I tried to get them to talk about it, but the only response I got was that I was mad, and Megan wanted no part of it. They would not accept I was tired, crabby, and wanted to be left alone. Suddenly, I was a bad guy again, and being blamed for the two-hour drive back to Sarah's. Not only that but Connie would not get to spend the extra time with the baby. Being optimistic and hopeful seemed to always end up costing me somehow. If I had learned anything, I should have learned to just stay clear of any situation with Megan. My instincts had been right, I should have not gone to Sarah's. That wrong decision cost me, and I paid heavily.

Maybe because everyone expected the day to end this way, it did. It became another shouting match that would be in the scorebooks as me being the worst man ever. Regrettably, I yelled at Megan that she had not changed at all. It was stupid and mean, and I wish I had kept my mouth shut. It seemed that other than that one phrase no one heard anything I had to say about being tired or crabby nor did they appear to care. I had to be and act like everyone thought I should. Oh, come on, is enough ever enough? I really hated this stuff. Not wanting to keep feeling that way, I, for the whatever time, wondered why I was still there. I tried to remind myself why had I not left years ago. Maybe I was whacky? Maybe I was just a coward. If only I had the guts to end this madness, my life and probably everyone's life would be calm, peaceful, and fun. I remembered the old plans I once had to move to Hawaii and be alone. Oh, how I wished I had stayed with those plans. If I had, I would have missed years and years of the ugliest things I had ever experienced. If I had, I would be relaxed, tan, and most likely sitting at the beach right this moment. The words, "If only" dominated my thinking the entire time Connie was gone. If only I had the courage to rent a car and drive back to South Carolina, she could stay in Ohio as long as she wanted, even forever for all I cared. She seemed to have finally joined the enemy's camp, so there was not much hope for me now. With her being on the other side now, I had nothing to lose. The rest I could figure out over time. It could be done. No fighting. No arguing. I could be packed and gone before she ever got back from Ohio. All it would take was getting a ride to the car rental place.

I called Sarah, trying to find out exactly what happened but ended up talking with her husband. I imagine Sarah was angry with me too, and it became another big family drama. A drama everyone had seemingly determined was my fault once more. Four plus hours later Connie returned, and we decided to talk it out.

Honestly, I really didn't want to talk it out. I was tired of talking. I was tired of the drama. I was tired of trying to prove myself worthy. Before I got myself into this mess, I was doing well. It seemed I was liked and respected by my friends and peers. It seemed I could accomplish anything I set my mind to. Now I had become a shell of that person. I was beaten down, weak, and had lost most of my own self-respect. I didn't think I could ever recover. I would never be anyone nor amount to anything ever again. I was a failure. I wished I could get a do-over and set the clock back years. I really didn't want to fix this, I wanted to escape this.

After we talked and days passed, I still could not stop wondering why I was still involved with this situation, why I was still here. It seemed apparent this family didn't really want any part of me.

You might be able to imagine how badly I wanted to have this part of my life over with. It was never over; it never changed no matter how hard I tried. Maybe God could find me a job in South America, so I would have a good reason to escape. I prayed and prayed for such an opportunity. I would be willing to go anywhere as long as it was far away.

For who knows how many times, I told Connie I was at my wits end. If I didn't act perfectly as everyone expected, I was evil, and the world exploded. I felt, for me, the bar had been set beyond reasonable expectations, and to make matters worse, it seemed I was the only one with a bar. It didn't appear to me anyone else had standards they were expected to live up to. It also seemed the family was turning on me. I hated every minute of it. Hated it, hated it, hated it!

That Easter went down in the journals as the one I wrecked for everyone. It was clearly the worst Easter I ever had, but it seemed what I felt didn't matter.

Back to South Carolina, back to normal life, and back to work. One thing I was not sure of though, I am not sure Connie and I had gotten back to normal. This time, there was something odd between us. Not big but different. Having had all this happen, I am not sure we would ever be the two people we were in California. We had not gone unchanged in all this.

It wasn't long before I started getting hang up calls. I knew from years of experience it was Megan. I ignored them because I had no desire to get into more arguments. Call after call, day after day, and I finally gave up and answered. Of course, it was Megan.

She started very calmly and controlled saying she was mad at me. I stayed calm and said, "Okay, why?" She said she was angry with me because of all the times I abused her. The horrible way she claimed I treated her was now causing her to be mean to her baby. I don't know what she meant by saying she was being mean to her baby. I did know, one, I had not abused her or beat her, and two, I was not going to be blamed for any such thing. I lost it and started defending myself and then the screaming started.

We screamed at each other at the top of our lungs. I told her that I never did anything to her, it was her fault her life is where it is, not mine. She was screaming things such as asking me if I liked being a child molester. Asking if there were a lot of little children in South Carolina for me to molest.

My mind snapped, and I was in a place mentally that I had never, ever been before. I was so angry and have no idea what I said in response to those comments, but I am sure I didn't hold back.

She threatened to call my work and tell them I was a child molester and threatened to call the police in California and South Carolina about me. Not having any idea what to do or how to respond, I just hung up.

I tossed my cell phone on the counter and started sweating and shaking, I was so angry. I spent my entire life trying to be a good guy. I loved people and especially kids. Never, ever could I ever hurt any little one. I wanted to hate this kid, I wanted to be free from her right now and for the rest of my life. I wanted her out of my life. I couldn't take this anymore. I prayed to once and for all be released from this terrible situation. Please set me free to find a new life. My life was the worst nightmare ever. I was gone this time, for real. If I had to give up my marriage to get away from Megan and her abuse, I would gladly do it.

All these years Megan claimed to be abused, but, in reality, it was Connie and mostly me who had been abused. All hours of the day and night, this child tortured us mentally and physically due to lack of sleep. She harassed us year after year, and she claimed abuse? How could anyone, especially a family member, twist things so out of proportion? How could she? I was about ready to go to California myself and confront her, dumping all the anger and disgust I felt for her in her lap. I could then leave this family forever and find my own way, doing the things I wanted, living where and how I wanted to live. I had enough.

Out of nowhere, I remembered a Scripture that tells us to pray for our enemies and for those who persecute us. It was Matthew 5:44 ESV; "But I say to you, Love your enemies and pray for those who persecute you." Nice thought but that was the last thing I wanted to hear. Forget that! I was angry, and I wanted to stay angry. So, I pushed that thought out of my mind. My heart was pounding harder than I had ever felt it pound. I had a pain in my chest and began wondering if I was having a heart attack. I was angrier than I had ever been and close to being filled with real hate. However, that Scripture would not leave me alone. As quickly and quietly as that Scripture again crept into my mind, a sense of peace crept in. I began settling down a little. I was filled with a rage that had now eased up a bit. It was as if the Lord was talking to me, helping me to get through this latest situation. I was sure I was going to end up in the hospital before this one was over.

Pray for her? It would be easier to explode and be gone. Oh, how I wanted to run. Eventually, even though I hated the idea, I let the Lord have His way with me, and I prayed for her without stopping. I prayed in desperation.

At first, I got angry, then forced myself to pray, then got angry again and prayed more. All the while I paced the living room trying to get rid of the feelings swelling up inside me. As I paced, I passed the huge windows revealing the palm trees that framed the path to the golf course. The beauty of this place was something I treasured, but even in this paradise, she had gotten to me. In that moment, I may have really hated her for the very first time.

After a few minutes, a new calmness came over me, and I settled down. I prayed good things for her, I prayed Scriptures over her, I prayed against the evil in her heart. I paced and prayed for at least thirty minutes. I don't know what it did for her, but I was completely filled with peace. He jumped in and redirected my thoughts, and I was blessed with His peace, a peace I could not understand. If it was hate I had really been feeling, even that had passed. It was okay, I could now breathe.

I never, ever want to feel that much anger and rage again. I vowed I would never talk to her again, ever. If Connie and I were to stay married, there was one condition she would have to agree to. She would have to understand I needed to have no contact with Megan whatsoever. She had to be out of my life. That one condition was not negotiable.

I told Connie she could visit Megan anytime she wanted, but they would have to meet at Sarah's or go to California, but I would never have her in our home. I needed a sanctuary, a place where Megan could not intrude. All these years, I wished her well, but now I didn't much care. She was not my friend, and I didn't want her in my life. It had to end, and this was the moment it would. If this plan was not acceptable, I would have no other choice than to leave. That was it, and I would not budge. That plan would have to be agreed to, or I would be gone by the end of the week. I was relieved to truly say what I was feeling. I held so much back all these years and felt a freedom in knowing she understood how I felt. Deep down, I hoped Connie would not agree to my conditions.

As I understand it, the mean things she said I made her do to her baby were, screaming at the baby when the baby was crying as well as throwing things across the room in anger because of the crying. Megan had some difficulties feeding the baby and had to use formula and other nutrients. It seemed those issues and frustrations are what provoked this new anger. Slowly, she seemed to lose patience with the baby and get angrier and more frustrated. The baby's crying increased because she was so hungry, and Megan had a hard time dealing with that. That was the situation that was all my fault. It seems there was very little that ever happened in this family that somehow was not my fault.

I supposedly made her act like that because I had been so mean to her. It seemed I was the cause of everything bad in her life. The thing was, I was never mean, stern yes, but not mean. I kept a tight rein on her because she was always off the deep end, but anything I did or said was always in response to what she did. Some of the time, Megan's initial actions were not all that bad, she might be out of line or annoying her sisters as kids do. It was her defiance and rebelliousness after any attempt to correct her that was off the charts. Her refusal to comply with direction from anyone is what always escalated to enormous fights. That being said, there was an amazing amount of times she came in intentionally gunning for a fight too. She knew right from wrong but appeared to like the excitement trouble brought.

Someone overheard Megan telling another person how she had acted toward the baby, and that person reported her to Child Services. Child Services investigated and took her baby from her. Luckily, they gave custody to Megan's father who had fallen in love with the baby. It was amazing to hear Connie talk about how much he loved the little one. Megan could see her at certain times but not be alone with her. Understandably, Megan was not happy about that, at all. It sounded like she dealt with it as well as anyone could.

Megan's father had the baby for two months during which Megan had to show her stability. She met all the requirements, and her baby was returned.

A bit later, her father bought her a condo, so she and the baby would never be homeless again. It was awesome to see her father do that for her. It had been a long road to this point, and he wanted them both to be safe. It was very generous and kind. It also gave me some comfort that her car would never again wear Ohio license plates.

I applaud him for that and all the other things he has done. I have seen it so many times that a dad completely disconnects from his kids. Her father had many reasons to do the same thing, but he didn't, and that was awesome.

My plan to stop any contact with Megan worked well for all of us. My world had become calm and peaceful, and Connie didn't have to be in the middle of all that fighting. She and Megan were enjoying a new, calmer relationship without me. I was enjoying not having any relationship with Megan. Something finally worked. Maybe I should leave and make this permanent. I was still looking for a way out.

Connie and I attended an event along the river in Savannah. Our friends took a couple pictures of us while we were there. We posted one of the pictures on social media showing Connie sitting on a hay bale. Admittedly, she looked tired from the long day. I stood beside her all tall and energetic. Megan saw the post and posted that picture proved that I was an abuser and it showed that I even abused Connie to the point she had no life left in her. Now I was abusing my wife according to Megan. I thought this was over. I had not communicated with her or had any interaction with her at all. I had stayed completely off the radar and away from her, yet she was after me again. There seemed to be no way to escape the ranting of this person. She also tagged me in that picture so that if anyone would pass their curser over me, an awful, disgusting word would appear instead of my name.

I was wordless. This kid just blasted me on public media for all my friends and anyone else out there to see. Katie, the daughter of friends of ours who grew up with Lizzie and often had sleepovers at each other's houses, went off on Megan and defended me. She really blasted her, and Megan did not even respond. I must say it made me smile. It seemed I had one much-needed ally. It seemed someone out there cared and was even willing to take a stand for me. Wow, that was something new and different. That was something I desperately needed.

In fulfilling my vow to never have contact with Megan again, I ignored her. Being proactive, I had to eliminate ways she could get to me, so I closed my online account, vanishing from cyber space. It was getting so I couldn't do anything. I had no privacy and had to consider how Megan might attack me using anything and everything I did. I was feeling I would never have any kind of a life. I was living, perhaps existing would be a more accurate word, in a box I had built out of a desperation to be unavailable for attack.

Connie was offered a job back in Ohio, so we moved. The move pushed the shoulder I injured when I fell on my motorcycle a couple years earlier, to its end. I was in pain so much of the time, it was wearing me down. Then winter hit, and it snowed, and I had to shovel snow. I was done. My shoulder failed, putting me in excruciating pain all day every day. I had no health care insurance but was blessed to be put on a low-income discount plan by the hospital. They were happy to take payments on the balance for the next year or so.

Over four years ago before moving to South Carolina, I fell with my motorcycle and seriously tore one shoulder and tore the other one as well but not as much. That first shoulder surgery was quickly followed by two wrist surgeries and one elbow surgery. Physically, or should I say structurally, I was fairly repaired but still had the non-repaired shoulder to one day get repaired. So, the failing of that shoulder and consequent surgery finished off all the ill effects of the motorcycle incident. Now, a year and a half after that final surgery, I was back in the gym. Being back in the gym was a welcome blessing. I had spent most of my life competing or working out, and this small pleasure had given me a sense of life being normal.

Connie got back to work while I looked for work with no success. Everyone told me to not move back to Ohio because the job market was poor, but we came anyhow. They were all right, finding a job was impossible. We have been back for a few years now and I still have had no luck finding employment. What I didn't know was it would be nine years before I could find even a reasonable part time job.

Following that one attack online, Megan seemed to settle down. She became quiet, and our life moved forward. She may have been quiet, but I knew she was always lurking in the background waiting for any opportunity to strike. I did not mistake the silence for a truce. It was only a ticking bomb waiting to explode.

We were in a new place where none of the awful things we had gone through in the past had been done. It was as if we were not living in the midst of a crime scene for the first time.

We lived in a peaceful little town with lots of nature around. We enjoyed hikes and bike rides and were content. We had gone back to our old church and were happy to see all those great people. Life had been good.

Well, it had been good until our phones started ringing in the middle of the night, again. You know the drill, call-no answer-hang up, call-no answer-hang up. We knew who it was, and we were off again.

I simply turned off my ringer. Connie ignored her calls and refused to talk to her. Time passed, and ever hopeful, Connie answered a call, but told

Megan she would not talk to her if she could not have a normal conversation. When Megan would start yelling at her, she would simply hang up. I think this just made Megan angrier, so she started another barrage of phone calls. We now turned off the phones before going bed. In the morning, we could turn the phones on and see how intense her calling had been.

One particular night, Megan started this assault on our cell phones trying to get into our phone management portion. Our passwords were easy to guess and guess them she did. She changed my password, so I could not retrieve any messages, and I would lose any ones I saved. She got into Connie's phone, changed the language to Spanish, and changed her password as well.

I got mine fixed quickly and then changed my phone number. It was a phone number I had for many years, and by making myself unavailable to Megan, I also lost touch with lots of people who knew that number. By changing it, hopefully, I took away the last possible way she could get to me. It had been pleasant knowing she could not harass me anymore. On the other hand, it was annoying that I had to live in hiding to avoid getting harassed. Connie's phone dilemma took three people at our cell provider to correct.

Here is an example of how crazed she would get. As verified by our cellular provider, one attack on our phones equated to Megan trying to access my phone management portion forty-five times in one hour and Connie thirty-nine times in an hour. It was obsessiveness at its worst. There had been times such attempts like that went on for days. We couldn't understand how anyone could do things like that. When I talk about how determined she was, I think this paints a clear picture for you.

What we didn't know was that the attack was not over so easily. Soon after the attack on our phones, Connie got a call from a Los Angeles Police Department detective. True to the threat she made years ago, she called LAPD. The detective called Connie investigating charges against me by Megan, accusing me of molesting her as a child. It seemed the threats she made to me when we were in South Carolina were not idle ones. We were both sick. After being married twenty-five years, we were still dealing with these attacks by Megan. All I needed was to have something like that show up on a background search sometime. How stupid was I to think that changing my phone number had finally protected me from any further attacks? Color me foolishly optimistic. Color her deviously determined.

We patiently worked through it with the detective, explaining what we endured all those years. She was kind and understanding, and I think even felt bad for us. When she had what she needed, she closed the case. At one point she asked why we had not pressed charges against Megan and suggested I should. Megan had broken laws and harassed us to the point of us being able to prosecute her. She advised us we were well within our legal rights to do so. My response was "What would be the point?" It would be like kicking a mean dog, it would only get meaner. Not only that but we hoped one day she would turn her life around. We wanted her to enjoy a good life like most people. We weren't out to punish her which may be why we managed to endure so much. Although, her treatment of us was well beyond anything we had ever heard of and now termed as violating laws, I wondered why we should keep trying. Years and years of our efforts to help her change did not seem to be working. What more would we have to experience before we gave up?

Do you remember me mentioning how many times she had gotten away with things and had never been held accountable? Here is another example of how some around us fell into the poor Megan way of thinking. During a discussion with a family member, we mentioned the detective's suggestion about filing charges against Megan. That person immediately became furious. We were being yelled at for thinking such a thing. There was little concern for what we had to live with or even that Megan was breaking the law. So many people bought into Megan the victim thing, giving us cause to feel as if we were in this mess all alone. Maybe filing charges was not such a bad idea after all. Should we take the detective's advice?

CHAPTER 13

Surrender?

With that last streak of meanness delivered by the episode with the phones and us being interviewed by the Los Angeles Police Department, I was again at that all too familiar wall. When I first met Connie, I was thirty-four and at this point I was nearing sixty-three. The problems with Megan started on our wedding day which was two months shy of twenty-seven years ago at this time, that being December of 1985. At this point, Megan was thirty-three. I share this information to give you an idea of how long this struggle has been going on. While these last ten years have not been every day occurrences, they still happen often. Often enough to keep me completely out of gas, and my well of hope was completely dry. It is odd as I say that because I have said I was done, worn out, out of gas, or all dried up so many times by now that I sound foolish. How can I say over and over, I was completely done, yet go on? How can I say over and over that leaving would be the best thing? There is absolutely no doubt in my mind it was simply a God thing.

We've prayed for years and years. We've prayed night after night for help and relief. We have sought out professional after professional to help us deal with this. I spent hundreds of hours talking with Megan, hoping to make an impact in her behavior and thought process. I have given up career opportunities to stay home to watch over the family.

Family got involved and tried to help. Even Connie's youngest brother spent hours on the phone talking to Megan, trying to help. I am confident there was no stone left unturned nor did we ignore any path that was presented to us. We searched, prayed, and begged that someone would find an answer to what was happening. We got answers, lots of answers, but they continued to be conflicting. We would try someone new, and our hopes would rise. We would be given an answer, and it didn't work, and our hopes would crash. We would find another option, and our hopes would rise only to crash again. Over and over this happened, but we kept trying. This up and down cycle was no joy ride, it was crushing. Yet, we tried and tried, but no one ever seemed to agree on the cause or problem. What choice did we have? Only one. Keep trying. We learned to try and not let new opportunities create high hopes nor to let failed attempts crush us. We began to do our best to stay at an even level no matter what. Sometimes we did well, other times we struggled.

I believed we would never have any sense of a normal life. I had become quite envious of all my friends who had life fall into place and move onto better and better things. I felt that God was answering prayers and fulfilling dreams for everyone but us. Our friends enjoyed life and looked forward to each new day while I sat bored, unemployed, miserable, and attached forever to some child, now adult, who seemed bent on my destruction.

This last attempt to hurt us was growing into the straw that broke my back. The fact that Connie and I were close to being married for twenty-seven years got my attention, reminding me I had the same concerns for a very, very, long time. Now I am really concerned I will be saying the same things another ten or fifteen years down the road. With all that is in me, I hope not. This new realization dominated my thoughts and filled me with fear.

Even with all the prayer, I felt as if God had not delivered, and I felt He had abandoned me. I often searched my past trying to find that big sin I committed, making Him unwilling to help. I know that is not how our God is, but there had to be an answer for our unanswered prayers. There had to be a reason for His silence.

Again, I was looking for an escape route out of this family and drama. Could I work out a plan that would give me a happy normal life while hurting as few people as possible? If I was to survive, it had to be done. I could not donate one more day to dealing with Megan. I had to stop letting this mess consume me and needed to start taking care of myself if there would ever be any chance of survival, if there would ever be any part of me left. Surviving was all I could focus on at this point. To hope for anything more would have to come later, if at all.

I found a sense of security in going off line and getting a new phone number and ending the episode with the Los Angeles Police Department.

I was hopefully unreachable and that was wonderful. I could not have felt better if I had won the lottery. I wanted to get on with my life and be completely detached from the life I had been living. I daily dreamed about a life alone and free from attack and drama. I wondered what it would feel like if I lived where no one knew who I was, and every day was a new adventure filled with calm and peace. I dreamt of being on my own and moving back to the beach. I could go back to Los Angeles, I had friends there. I could go back to South Carolina and had friends there as well. Both locations offered me the beach life I loved.

Every time I considered leaving, I meant it. In my flesh and heart, I was terribly desperate. The more I contemplated a move, the more I believed it would be the right thing for me, but I also knew it would be the wrong thing overall. Thinking about it now, I wonder if the thing holding me back was some mental or emotional issue. Why was I here? Why should I stay? What did I have left to give? What was I getting out of it? Didn't I deserve better than this? Didn't I deserve something good? I didn't have any answers to those questions. Questions that I must have asked myself dozens of times over the years.

You know how it is in times of stress. You deal with the issues, and you merely try to squeak out fun and joy whenever and wherever you can. That is what I did. I repaired things around the house, cut the grass, and did whatever I could do to occupy my mind. It was like being in a busy, joyless coma.

Years back, when the battles were every day, every holiday, every vacation, every get together, I had to be in full battle mode. Picture a soldier in the heat of battle as it rages on and bullets are flying everywhere all the time. All you can think of is surviving and doing your job as a soldier. I think that is where I was. Lately, the war had died down, yet there were still skirmishes here and there. Just enough to let me know the enemy was alive and plotting attacks. That is what I needed to get away from. I needed to get away from worrying about when the next outbreak would occur. I wanted to quit jumping when the phone rang, I wanted the war to be over. My enemy was relentless. As I have said many times, I feared it would never be over.

What I did not want to have happen was to see ten more years go by and me still be living this way. Filing charges against her was still an idea, but leaving would be easier and do less damage.

I asked God if I did something to deserve this and other questions with, of course, no answer. I hated to surrender, but if surrender was what I had to do to escape the pain and suffering, then surrender it would be. In my heart and head, I was waving the white flag and telling God I was done and had nothing more to give. All I needed was a plan.

While that simmered on the back burner of my brain, life continued. We had been able to enjoy some time with friends, and enjoy each other. I had relaxed a bit when not dealing with the stomach issues that had come back.

We had become more involved at our church. We even were blessed to work with the fourth-grade class and what a joy those kids were. It took me back to when I had the highest of expectations for the little family I wanted to help make whole. The sweet faces of the fourth graders were always happy to see you, they were eager to give hugs, and their sensitivity and realness was inspiring. I have always loved kids and still do even after a nearly twenty-seven years of struggles with one of them. The chance to be part of the summer classes brought back the joy I had felt for kids most of my life.

As an uncle, I loved annoying my nieces and my "favorite nephew," (although I have only one nephew that doesn't change anything, he is still my favorite! HA). I loved wrestling with them, tickling them until they screamed for mercy, and letting them pile on Uncle Rick until he surrendered. Now they are grown, although I still see them as little ones, I enjoy adult conversations about their plans and dreams. Kids are just awesome and have been a big part of my life. Their giggles and laughter have filled my heart for years. With that being said, we and the kids in our class grew fond of each other, and often, when they wanted a hug or to be close, those lying and hateful words of Megan's proclaiming me to be an abuser and molester robbed me of the joy the kids brought. I was super sensitive and careful to never be in any situation that could ever be misinterpreted.

We attended a wonderful church that was full of activity. Weekend services were great, praise and worship were amazing, and the people that make up the church were fabulous. They really were a great big family. Since coming back to Ohio and going back to our old church, it had been an oasis that had given me some comfort and rest.

One of our traditions was to have a week of prayer a couple times a year. They set aside a week for anyone who could come to church to pray together as a group. We prayed for the direction of the church, the staff, local and governmental issues, and whatever else was on our minds. It was also a time to offer prayers of thanksgiving for answered prayers and blessings.

There was a prayer leader at each session three times a day for a week.

For as long as we had been attending this church, I tried to make as many sessions as possible.

I was good at making all of them until one particular year. That year I was happy to make one a day because we had moved farther away.

Something I always did during the week of prayer was to ask God what it was He wanted me to learn and to take away with me. I remember one year, I prayed for an answer to that question twice a day for the entire week. Patiently I waited for the lesson I was to come away with. At the end of the last prayer session, I had not yet received an answer. I decided to wait for God another ten minutes, and while everyone left, I sat and waited. God touched my heart with the thought I was to be the most thankful man I could be. That led to some incredible insight and prayers of thanksgiving.

I admit, I have fallen quite a bit short of being as thankful as I was following that week of prayer. Hopefully, I will once again recognize how blessed I am. I had let myself become consumed by the troubles of life and of the issues with Megan. I had become the best man of moaning and complaining I could be, spewing prayers of what about me.

I especially looked forward to the next week of prayer this time, and we did our best to make a fun forty-minute trip of it. Sometimes we would stop for coffee or visit with friends following the meeting.

One particular evening, we gathered in the sanctuary while our session leader went over all the requests of the church and other personal prayer concerns left by others. I had a whisper of a thought. It was one of those spiritual moments that you feel is the nudging of the Holy Spirit. I raised my hand and asked the leader if I might have a few minutes in front of the group. I understood once I told my story, my entire life would then become public knowledge. I had to choose either to do what I spirituality believed needed to be done or choose to selfishly protect my name. I knew what had to be done and did it.

Unprepared, I stood before that group of friends and bared it all. I talked about my stepdaughter who had overdosed several times, had called me an abuser, accused me of being a child molester, and who had waged war on me for years.

I talked about wanting to hate this kid with all the humanness I had, but could not. I shared I had given up any idea of ever having a normal relationship with Megan and was just trying to do the best I could with life and stay out of her way. I told them how we prayed for her all these years and that how I had come to feel that my prayers just didn't seem to have enough clout with God to make a difference. I asked them if while they were praying, they would pray for my stepdaughter Megan.

I told them I was not asking for a great relationship with her, nor anything for me. What I asked them to pray was that something in her life would change, that someone would come alongside her, and that she would have a normal, happy life. I needed help because my prayers alone had yet to get the job done. We broke into groups and went into our prayer time.

I believe they all prayed with open hearts and with a pure spirit. We prayed as one heart with a united focus for Megan to have a good and normal life. I left that prayer session absolutely sure, "NOW" I have finally done everything I could do. I felt I truly had nothing else to give or do.

The calm continued when two weeks later, Connie had an opportunity to talk to Megan. Connie finished her conversation with Megan and told me she was so excited that Megan sounded normal. Phone call after phone call was the same, she sounded normal. Megan's best run of normal, not including the pregnancy and having the baby, never went longer than ten days. At this writing, it has been nearly nine months that she has been normal.

We believe that God answered the church group's prayers nine months earlier on that awesome night along with all our years of prayers. That night He made something happen in her life. That night God moved, and the world changed.

Within days of our week of prayer, Megan turned back to attending church and reading the Bible. She told Connie that she had often felt so evil inside and had come to a discovery. She understood for her to keep the darkness she felt away from her, she had to read the Bible first thing in the morning and the last thing at night before going to bed, every day. She said she knew God was changing her life.

That very statement reminds me of a Scripture found in Matthew 19:26 (NIV); Jesus looked at them and said, 'With men this is impossible, but with God all things are possible.'" We all know Jesus was not talking about Megan, but the truth of the matter was the same. We did everything we could possibly do for so many years and nothing ever changed, nothing ever gave Megan a life nor us peace.

It seems we had to get to the place where all we could do was admit we had nothing left. We kept seeing what we thought was Megan hitting bottom, and each time we saw her get to that place, we had hope. However, it was never the bottom, and it continued to get worse.

Maybe it was us who had to hit bottom. Maybe our efforts and determination had to fail completely before we could earnestly ask for help.

We did. We failed. We hit bottom. We played our last card. We asked God with all our hearts to step in and save her from the life she had been living. God did what we could not do. We cannot take credit saying that our prayers did it, because we offered hundreds of prayers, yet nothing changed. While typing that last line, I realized something did change. Our self-reliance and need for God changed greatly. Our hearts were fully open to tell Him how much we needed Him. Our hearts were also fully open to receive the blessing of what He was about to give. In fact, we longed for His blessing for at this point it was our only hope.

This time God moved, and I cannot tell you why this time except that we absolutely had no place to turn. He moved quickly and powerfully and gave this grown child a future and a hope which brings me to another Scripture found in Jeremiah 29:11 (NIV), "'For I know the plans I have for you,' declares the Lord, 'plans to prosper you and not to harm you, plans to give you hope and a future.'"

God was talking about ending the exile of Judah and restoring Judah in this Scripture. I believe it applies today in many things. I believe nothing escapes God's watchful eye, and that He always had plans for Megan, plans of prosperity, hope, and a future.

I guess I should feel lucky, Judah was in exile for seventy years, Megan and I only had to deal with this for twenty-seven years.

When I made plans to write this book, I always saw it ending with words something like, "This is one story that doesn't have a happy ending." In fact, when I wrote out what I would say on the back cover of the book, I said exactly that. The turn of events at the hand of God was not what I ever thought would happen. While I am overwhelmed with happiness, I am also in awe of our loving and awesome God.

God had a plan. Reflecting on all these events and all this time, if God had given Megan a normal life after only two or three years, would I be as in awe of Him? Would I want to tell you of His greatness? Would I even notice what a powerful thing He had done? I don't think I would have. Certainly, this book would only have shared my disappointments not His glory.

The old saying is, "Anything worth having is worth waiting for." I have waited, and it is worth it. God is good, praise be to God. It seems recently God has connected Megan to a doctor who analyzed her issues and prescribed a medication that has worked very well. I say that with a hearty "finally'.

Finally, Megan will have a life that all our children should have, and we will have a life of freedom from conflict and accusation. Finally, it is finished. With what feels like my biggest sigh ever, finally.

It was a difficult lesson, but we learned when we had really given up any hope of doing anything on our own, God acted. In fact, He acted three times we are sure of. The other two times were when we as a family were united in prayer for protection for Megan. Prayer is powerful and amazing. God can do amazing and mighty things. Never give up on Him.

CHAPTER 14

No More, Please

Things settled in nicely. Life was as close to normal as it had been so far back that I could barely remember. If you think about it, I had gone from a thirty-something guy to an early sixties guy and lost many, many years of life filled with what many people take for granted.

Connie continued talking with Megan on the phone regularly. I had started a Christian-based website and blog which was expanding and kept me writing. The website was getting about 800 views a month at that time. That seeming success made me feel like I had a new purpose which did not include defending myself or fighting off feelings that I was a miserable person. That writing would be validated years down the road as my site grew to getting 17,000 views a month.

My body had been hurting a great deal, even so, I was working out fairly regularly in the basement with a couple dumbbells, some straps, and a tube set. I was getting stronger but was an extremely far cry from the shape I was in when I was competing as a bodybuilder. I knew from all the years of lifting that I had to take baby steps and be patient in restoring my body to any level of fitness. I also knew I had to accept the thought it would never be what it once was.

Life was calm without the threat of what might rear its ugly head from California. We enjoyed cycling in the park, hiking, and sitting in the backyard gazing at the flames skipping over all the wood in our fire pit. While sitting around the fire, it was so easy to get lost in thought and sometimes even start to dream of our lives finally becoming something like our friends were enjoying and something to be excited about. We were actually beginning to consider the future rather than dedicating all our thoughts to how we were going to survive the present.

We enjoyed more and more time with friends and had gotten some of our bills handled, giving us a little room to entertain ourselves.

Megan's miraculous breakthrough by God's gracious hand, encouraged us all. The well of hope that had been completely dry for so very many years was now filling up with new hopes and dreams. Trying to remember when life was this easy was, well, near impossible.

Megan had her daughter in pre-school three times a week, she was walking for exercise, taking only a very small amount of prescription medication, and she seemed bright, hopeful, and excited for the future. Connie often thought maybe the struggles Megan had were hormonal rather than mental, but that had never been explored. Considering most of the medication made her worse, I agree.

It was difficult to believe that we had traveled nine months without an issue. There were no nasty calls, threats, complaints, or accusations. I never thought we would go that long with that much peace.

God can and does do amazing things, but we can choose to do things to wreck what He has done, and she was doing just that.

With nine months of peace behind us, Megan began having anger issues again. God only knows why, but she had begun drinking large amounts of wine daily. She had set aside her reading of the Bible, God time stopped, and she had fallen back into being entombed by thoughts of her so-called horrible life. She was having a difficult time dealing with her daughter. As the little one became more and more active, she required more and more of Megan's time and effort, something she did not have in her to give at that point.

Megan called Connie several times with the same old story about what a disgusting person I was. Megan never really gave much thought to the idea that by now Connie was sick and tired of hearing her husband being torn down. Connie listened patiently, tried to calm Megan, but would not agree with the comments and anger.

For the next five months we would find Megan phasing in and out of being under control. One week she would be fine, the next she would be lecturing Connie on how bad I was and how horrible her life had been and is. It appeared to me, Megan had been battling and plotting my exit since she was very little. I guess to her, life had always been pretty bad. We had battles and struggles all these more recent years, but it wasn't a daily thing like it was when she got into her teenage years. Those years were tough, extremely tough. Those years were filled almost daily with hours and hours of shouting and arguing and bad behavior. Those were the combative years when she was still living in our house full time, and also later as she checked in and out of the old Reeder motel as needed. These more recent years had battles but not nearly as frequent. While less frequent, the issues and level of drama was much higher.

Adding to our mounting stress, it was now June. We had been renting the house we were living in for close to two years when we got an email from the owner of the house. Due to a career change, the owner was moving back to town and needed her house back. We were fortunate to have received two-months' notice, giving us until August first to be out. That meant packing up the entire house for the fifth time in five years. Because of our limited finances, every move had for the most part been me doing the majority of the packing, loading, and unloading, and I was getting tired. Very tired.

We had two months to look, but even so, we were frantic. The rental market in the area was poor and pricey compared to what we had seen in South Carolina. We looked all over the area and spent every spare minute searching ads, looking at real estate web sites, and asking everyone we knew about a house for rent. It sounds a bit like the rental fiasco we had years ago. Hurry and be out with no prospects for a new place was the same situation we had dealt with then and here we were at it again. Last time we ended up in a newly built home designed just for us. I doubted that would happen again.

I was taking this as an opportunity, maybe even a "sign" to move back to South Carolina but that was a move Connie and I did not agree on. Bummer, a guy can hope can't he. Man, I miss the beach. Living here in the middle of the country was squashing me. The beach and ocean always gave me peace and strength, and I dreamt it would once again be available to me.

Fortunately, within a month, we found a new place. This house was one we had admired since we moved back to Ohio. It had never been for rent, and we knew nothing about it. Being able to rent it was as big a shock as the news we had to move was. It was a much-needed blessing, and we began packing. The great thing was that it was only a couple blocks from where we had been living, making the packing easier, and the drive time a non-issue.

With the help of friends and family, it only took a couple days of running our belongings to the new place. I spent another two weeks getting everything unpacked and put away. Two weeks passed, and again we were settled in another new house. It all happened so fast it felt unreal. I was kind of dazed for another week and felt out of place. Even though we only moved a couple blocks, the rhythm of our lives was off and would take a little time to adjust.

Sarah, her husband, and all the grandkids called with plans to visit the new place for a weekend. It was early August, and a perfect time to have them visit. It had been hot, anywhere from 80 to 100 degrees most of the summer, but the weekend they came was chilly.

We went to the park nearby so the kids could climb on all the cool park stuff and swing on the swings. We ate all manner of junk intertwined with a few nutritious meals. We went to Lizzie's house, so we could all swim in her pool. We swam but froze as that was the coolest day of all. We cooked out and went back to our house.

Lizzie posted on a social media website how great it was to have her family visit and hang out. Apparently, Megan saw the post and was enraged. After all those past months of "normal," she turned mean again. None of us knew that was going on until I checked my website and saw this post by Megan; (unedited except for deleting a name and manufacturer, copied and pasted from my site.)

"I see how you are trying to save the abused animals and broken families and you said in 1992 your life changed dramatically. That you felt the need to show God's love. Let me ask you this then is cornering your 16 yr old stepdaughter into the mud room and smacking her 6 to 7 times in a row on her thigh is that showing "GODS LOVE"? Or calling her a moron, nimrod, (curse word blanked out) or telling her she going to be in Hell while the rest of the family will be looking down from Heaven waving to her? Or telling her that she should wear a purple or black dress on her wedding day? Or what about that time in your white (XXXXX) truck with your friend (XXXXX) and she was 5 ...What happened? why does she feel like she was fondled by your friend? you guys gave her ice cream after? You still haven't admitted to all this and when she say these things to you ..you yell back and talk over her? THIS IS NOT LOVE ITS ABUSE...THATS WHY GOD WONT LET YOU PASTOR A CHURCH....YOU ARE A FRAUD....A FAKE.. AND NEVER AMOUNTED TO ANYTHING....YOUR LIFE WAS MEANINGLESS..YOU ARE THE LOSER!"

I am not going to spend the time it would require to argue all her comments. If I was afraid they were true, I surely would not have shared them here. All I will say is that we had conversations on some of the things, but her interpretations are radically skewed and others are just untrue. That being said, in doing this I also am allowing her thoughts to be shared as well as my own.

I will use one of her comments here to show how frustrating and difficult it was to communicate with her. Her mind would seem to think things and then those thoughts would be seen as having been said by someone else. Let me share the thing about wedding dresses.

I was in my office at home when Megan came in and wanted to talk. I stopped working, as always, and gave her my undivided attention. She may have been thinking about getting married as all girls do now and again, and she wanted to know what the white wedding dress was all about.

My response was something like, traditionally, women wear white wedding dresses for their first wedding if they were virgins. Remember this discussion was many years ago, and now days that doesn't seem to always be the tradition. I told her about her mom, who had been married before and had kids and that she wore a cream-colored wedding dress. In fact, it was a beautiful dress not even really what you would think of as a wedding dress.

That was basically the discussion. You have read her comments that I told her she would have to wear black or purple, which is nothing I ever said, not even anything I ever thought. I talked about cream and how other colors would be fine too. Maybe her mind conjured up the thought that she was so bad that she had to wear black. In reality, she attacked me for saying something that wasn't said during that conversation. It may have come up at another time when her feelings may have led her to those thoughts, but not something I would have told her she should do.

I know this seems like a small thing, and it really is. The part that is so difficult is how things jumped from something simple to something that she claims as abusive and mean. It seemed we could only have a few conversations that didn't end up like that one. To get a post like the one I am talking about many, many years after the conversation and never having any idea she thought such things, made it impossible to clarify for her. If she had gone down that road about black dresses and either talked with me about it or even accused me of the comment long ago, maybe I could have straightened it out.

The problem with wishing that she would have shared her thoughts with me a long time ago was, as I mentioned elsewhere, once she took something in right or wrong, it was locked in and I was a bad person.

I may have called her a brat, ungrateful, or accused her of lying, but calling her some of the names she accused me of using makes no sense. Like nimrod, I don't even know what that is and never heard it until she mentioned it. Such vocabulary may have come out in the heat of battle, but none of the rest of the family remembers it. If it had, it would be the result of my anger and frustration but not part of my typical normal vocabulary.

You need to remember there was three or four people around most of the time and never less than two. If I had called her some names, there would be witnesses. There are witnesses, but they are witnesses to the fact I didn't talk like that, and no one remembers me calling her such names. Although, I can imagine it would have been easy for me to think such things.

As for the leg thing, I shared that event with you earlier. I hate to even think of that moment, it was one of the ugliest moments ever. It is certainly not my best moment. I feel like a fool for acting that way and a fool for being drawn into such a situation. Along with the laundry room incident and pushing her onto her bed once, this was the third of three such physical confrontations we had. I am not proud of those moments and sincerely wish they had not happened.

Last, I never told her she was going to hell, and all the family would be in heaven waving to her. In fact, I worked hard to help her understand quite the opposite. There was a time she called me scared and emotionally panicked that she was going to hell. I was driving and pulled over and sat in a parking lot for over an hour convincing her she was not going to hell.

Here I was, doing a site to encourage people, and it had been nicely followed for eight months at that point. I wanted to give up on the site simply to avoid giving her any opportunity to slander me. I am so happy I didn't give up in fear of other possible comments she might post.

She harassed me on the internet, on a public site for all the world to see. I was in shock but not angry, furious, or hurt. I simply deleted her comments from the site. I was not experiencing any of the other emotions I had felt in the past when being abused by her. That in itself was a blessing and a gift from above.

What do you think you might feel after experiencing things such as this for nearly twenty-seven years? This time I didn't get the feeling I wanted to leave. This time I didn't have the need to be done with it all and run away. Does any of that make any sense to you?

The family had a great time visiting, but I was kind of deflated. There was nothing by me or about me in the post made by Lizzie, just that she had a great time with her family. For a long time, I had no direct contact nor any communication at all with Megan, and still she went after me. She attacked me about a post not done by me and one not even mentioning me. I have never understood why she did that and do not to this day. I can understand her feeling left out or even angry she wasn't there to spend the day. Maybe she thought I was what prevented her from doing such fun things. Even so, she was still living in California and would never be able to simply pop in for a fun day. I am not attempting to justify what she did. I am just saying it makes absolutely no sense to me for her to keep going after me for such things.

Incorrectly, I was sure all such issues were behind us, and in complete disappointment, we found that it had again simply been dormant. I prayed … no more please!

I chose to share her post with the family while they were still here. You might imagine how angry everyone got. I suggested no one retaliate or get angry. I asked them to let it go and move on. They were just words, and the only power they had was the power we gave them. The attack and attempt to upset me fizzled. I was a little proud of myself for that. This time I was not hurt, angered, or demoralized. Our visit returned to normal, and we had a wonderful time.

Two days later, I checked my website again and found another post by Megan. Foolishly, I believed that the first attack had satisfied her, and it was over with. I was wrong, and I was shocked.

Here is her second post; (unedited, copied, and pasted from my site)

> "Ok you are such a fake...Those are true accusations that you continue to deny....You make a website to boost your self esteen since you are not usefull for society these days... All those people who follow your wesite are TOTALLY oblivious to you're wanna be a pastor but wont happen talk...

> "Oh God showed me this and God showed me that" is hypocracy....God did not tell you to abuse me did he? NO satan did and you listened to him for years and you abused me mentally and physically for YEARS...

Its OK GOD is taking care of me and HAS been because HE saw how i was treated...

YOU ARE LIAR and you have everyone believing you....."

Actually, she was the one who was not truthful, and she was the one who at one time had family and friends believing her. Again, I was not devastated. Again, I simply deleted it and then blocked her from the site and never acknowledged either comment.

Let me remind you that everyone including a court appointed social worker found all her accusations to be unfounded and untrue. Let me remind you of that Easter when she called the entire family and admitted she lied about everything, including abuse. Let me also remind you in her first comment on my site, in her own words she said she felt like my friend fondled her. There is no mention of him assaulting her, nor of me doing anything at all. Let's go back to her comment after the day we drove my friend home. Remember, she said she felt his penis while sitting on his lap. That was it. That was her only comment, and she told me about it as soon as we returned home from dropping my friend off. I believe that is the real truth, and I also believe the rest of the stories are fabrications stemming from that incident.

Sure, we argued and often. When I would try to explain or give some guidance, she would begin rattling off words that flooded the room like the rapids in a river. I could not get a word in at all. I felt like I was drowning in her volume of words and to survive I had to shout louder. It seemed to never matter though because I believe she never heard a thing I said. I tried to make allowances for her, considering she had been evaluated and was determined to be in need of medication and has been on and off medication for many years.

Could have I been a better parent to her? Knowing what I know now, I believe I could have been a great deal better, but at that time, we had no concept of what we were dealing with. As it was, even the doctors had no idea what was going on or how to help. Some of it may have been her chemistry, and some of it may have been her attitude. Doctor after doctor, psychologist after psychologist, psychiatrist after psychiatrist, no one ever came to the same conclusion. No one had been able to help her or us. As much of a horrible life she claims hers was, ours was as well. She endured some arguing and some loss of privileges and a swat here and there. We spent so much of so many days doing research on how to help her. We talked with doctors and took her to professionals over and over again.

All of our efforts to help Megan were always met with resistance. Such efforts were never met with appreciation or cooperation. She never expressed any desire to do things differently nor was she willing to make any effort to resolve issues. She fought us at nearly every attempt to make this family right.

Years and years of our lives had been completely consumed by trying to help this girl get help. Do the other kids share any of her sentiment? No, of course not, nor do they recall the so-called horrible life she claims. Even though they were innocent victims in this chaos, they don't think of those years as terrible. The only parts of those years they remember as being bad were the times Megan would rant and rave and turn our home upside down. How could someone hang on so long? How could she continue year after year to be so hurtful? Was this madness? Isn't there anyone who can help us?

Someone recently asked us why we didn't have her institutionalized. Fair question. We had her in many treatment programs as you have read, but at the time there was absolutely no place that would take a person with her history. There was no place that was set up to deal with people with her issues. The only things out there that could potentially help us were the psychologists and medications, and as you saw, those didn't work out so well. We were on our own figuring it out as we went. The fact there was no help gave us feelings of hopelessness and the burden of never being able to stop searching and researching. So much time was spent trying to make sense of all this and we never have.

If only there had been a place that could have taken her in and helped her. If only there had been professionals who knew how to deal with her. If only I had gone to Hawaii. If only we had more money to get her better help. It took time, but we learned "if only" doesn't get you anywhere. It was what it was, and we had to hang in there and do our best. We had to do our best no matter how long it took.

CHAPTER 15

Awakened

It had been a couple months since the last episode. Still I lived just doing my best to stay out of her way and was basically trying to, more or less, be invisible. Connie continued to talk with her and tried to guide her.

Megan was regularly seeing a counselor which was good news. My only fear was that the counselors can only deal with what information they are given. In all the years we have been in this struggle, she has been the only one giving information to the doctors and psychologists. The sad thing is while they may be able to help and get her past all this, they may end up giving less help than they could if they knew all the truth.

In my mind the biggest roadblock to her making progress is that I have never heard her take responsibility for anything in her life. She blames me, at times her father, and other times her mother for her situation. In her mind it seems to have always been our fault that her life is what it is. She has made hundreds of poor decisions that have no root in our years of conflict, yet even the cause of those decisions seems to be blamed on her awful childhood.

The encouraging thing was when she seemed to accept the idea she needed help and medication. Her coming to that place did not happen all at once. She seemed to have edged into a more complete level of acceptance overtime. She seemed to have begun the path to acceptance as a result of the week of prayer. She accepted the advice then but wandered away. She came back to accepting that life could be pretty normal when she had been strict with her medication. Her willingness to listen to a professional and take medicine was a huge thing in our opinion. Without it we feel as if her life would never change. We feared she would never have any chance of a normal life - nor would we.

As for us, we are doing okay. We pray for her, we hope for her, as we have for twenty-nine years now, that she will have a wonderful family and a normal life. We want to see her succeed, prosper, and once and for all, stop living this roller coaster of a life. Years have flown by, and they have been wasted. We hope and pray that her life will grow into something amazing. The crazy thing about all of this is that she has the intelligence, charisma, and ability to make anything she wants of her life. We have seen moments of such potential over and over again. It seems as if life falls into a normal forward moving place, she gets tired of it, and looks for excitement, or for someone else to make it better for her. Then she throws all her hard work away and has to start all over again.

As I mentioned earlier, Megan had been living in a condo her father owns. She lived there with her young daughter. She had a car and everything she needed. She was being helped in financial and medical matters by her state, and life was not bad. Megan called to tell her mom she had sold her car and everything she could. She told her she was leaving her daughter with her father and had bought a round-trip ticket to Morocco and was leaving for a few weeks to see if things could work out there. The thought of another trip to Morocco tired me out so much so that I don't even want to look back to see what plan letter we left off with. You all know she had made that trip many times with the same result, she comes back.

We have prayed so often that this very cycle would be broken. It seems this type of thing just drives her life to crash again and again. This present plan to go to Morocco was not her last. One more plan to go there was to come, but thankfully, neither one was ever acted on.

Connie was crushed again. She was completely against Megan going to Morocco and called her mother and family and asked them not to help Megan with money or anything but to pray for her. Connie's mom was so upset, she called Megan and basically yelled at her. Megan called Connie and yelled at her for telling Grandma. Megan responded once again with the anger and fury she had so often displayed over all these past years toward the world's worst mom. Connie and Megan's father talked a bit, and it appeared the family was all in agreement that this was a foolish mistake. Megan was in her thirties so what can anyone do except try to help her make a decision that would not destroy her entire world yet again?

Megan's father was finally able to convince her that her plan was foolish, and she eventually got a refund on her airline ticket and stayed. This was a huge victory, and hopefully was a sign that she was starting to think in a better way. In a moment, she planned to leave everything behind, even her daughter temporarily, to follow what seemed like an impulsive thirst for change and excitement. Maybe more truthfully, it may be a search to feel valued and loved.

Her continual searching kept missing what was right in front of her. There were many around her that loved her, but rather than accept the love they offered, she tried to tell them "how" to love her. And lastly, the love anyone offered her was never "good" enough. She seems to continue to look for love, but I think she may never recognize it until she learns to love herself. Once she does, I believe her world will be a very different place.

I wish we had earlier come to understand she needed to learn to love herself, mistakes and all. If we had, we could have done all we could to help her see it and learn to do just that.

Things suddenly changed as the result of a difficult time in all our lives. It was just before Thanksgiving about two years ago. As we were nearing our home after being down south visiting friends, Connie received a call from her brother. Their dad was ill and not doing very well, and his suggestion was we get to Chicago as soon as possible. We repacked the car and headed to Chicago. We, along with her brothers, their wives, Mom, and some grandchildren managed to be there in time to spend some time with Dad before he passed away. It all happened in a matter of a couple days.

We scurried back to Ohio for Thanksgiving and immediately back to Chicago for his funeral. The funeral and tributes to Dad were amazing and comforting. We stayed with Mom a bit as she received visitors and well-wishers.

Most of what you have read so far has been about our struggles in our relationship with Megan. What you will see in the next few pages is not what we had to deal with but what Megan and her dad had to deal with. At this time, we were out of the range of fire and mostly just observers. It was so hard to watch a person you tried so hard to help continue to have her life crash over and over again. For a time, it seemed like she was actually building a normal life with only a few stumbles while also experiencing some consistency.

I imagine you may remember me mentioning earlier how it seemed every holiday and vacation was negatively impacted by Megan. The day of the funeral was no different. Upon hearing the news of Connie's dad's passing, Megan overdosed one more time. Although, this time it was not like the others. This time it was not an effort to control or threaten us nor to hurt herself. This time she legitimately could not deal with Grandpa's death. She loved Connie's mom and dad greatly and was so overwhelmed with his passing she couldn't handle it. This indeed was the last overdose as of the end of this book.

Child services heard about what she did, and she came so very close to having her daughter taken from her. Her father stepped in and took temporary custody to protect the little one from being placed in the system. For a second time, he would maintain custody until Megan was once again stable. This time, they would not put her back on the same bipolar medicine she overdosed with. Becoming stable without drugs was an extremely difficult time for her. As time passed, they did prescribe a different set of medications.

It seems she had been drinking again when her grandpa passed away. I heard she would drink a 1.5-liter bottle of wine at one sitting. Eventually, Megan saw how the drinking had a hold on her and again began working with Alcoholics Anonymous. She was determined to get sober and stay that way. She was determined to get her life back. She was becoming responsible and self-reliant, and that was all good. She was even taking responsibility for her life.

Sometime during all this, she met a man and they started dating. He is bipolar and was still crushed by his wife committing suicide less than a year earlier. They seemed to really care for one another and loved spending time together which eventually turned into a fairly serious relationship. Megan had been in the AA program less than a year when things got serious, and it most likely was not a good decision to begin a relationship while she was still working on overcoming her drinking.

A few months into the relationship, they began having issues with some things, and their relationship began to struggle. After eleven months of being sober and being in AA, things between them got very strained and appeared to be falling apart. Megan responded to their problems by stopping her medications and went right back to drinking. Megan was struggling and was in one of the darkest times of her life. She could no longer handle her daughter who ended up staying with Megan's father full time.

Her father and his wife went back to court and legally received full temporary custody of Megan's daughter. Megan knew she was in no shape to give her little one the care she deserved and was happy things worked out that way with her father. She had been very depressed for a very long time but began pushing herself to get straightened out. On her own initiative, she began counseling sessions and was put on a new set of medications. These new medications seemed to cause her great anxiety, something she had never dealt with in the past and something we had never seen in her.

There were still battles; however, the battlefield had changed. We have not been in any battle with her for years now. Megan's battle had now become a battle with herself. Happily, it seemed she really wanted life to change. It seemed like she had grown tired of how she was living, and she seemed determined to finally get it all right. She talked of how she believed she had to tough it out, stay on the medication, and be obedient to the doctors. With a few exceptions, she had not blamed any of us for anything. It seemed she had been taking responsibility for her actions and dealing with them. We had never seen her like this. This was what we had been waiting to see. She blamed everyone around her for so long, but now she seemed to know it was all on her. Yay for her. We were so proud of her.

Sometime after she sold all her things and gave up on the Morocco idea, her father sold the condo and put her in a place he had on his property. That was a great thing. She was close to help if she needed it, and her daughter could be well cared for.

Those two years had brought very little arguing with us and a great deal of hope. We had seen an amazing amount of growth in Megan and believed she was truly on the right path to a new and much better life. The only struggle we had in all this was watching her go through some of the hardest times she had been through. She had the right mind set and was determined to make it this time, and we were all in her corner. Her efforts to follow the doctors' instructions had put her in the deepest, scariest place I had seen her go. But she kept hanging on believing and hoping in someone other than herself. Finally, after several months of the most horrifying anxiety I had ever witnessed, Megan told the doctors she could not take any more of this.

She has not blamed anyone. Now, it seems she has taken it upon herself to make things right. I believe she will not give up this time. I believe she will push through to the good life she deserves.

The change in the medication took some time, but after a couple recent conversations Connie had with Megan, Megan seems to really have it all together. The medicine they put her on is the same thing the doctors gave her so many years ago when she had her longest streak of normal life. Megan is now spending time every day with her daughter and seems so positive about the future.

Megan has lived most of her life in anguish and despair. She has survived.

She has endured, and I believe the very best is yet to come. We have never been so hopeful nor would we have ever been willing to wager on her not relapsing again. We are proud of the path she has decided to take and are all very optimistic.

Fast forward another year, and Megan is doing great. She is working part-time, still with her boyfriend, going to counseling, and free of alcohol and medications other than ones prescribed for her.

We have seen that when God gets involved, He never stops working no matter how many bad decisions we make. He never gives up no matter how long it takes. When He starts working in a person's life, He is in it until the end.

We also have seen that no matter what we wanted, no matter what we tried to do, Megan had to come to the place where she wanted a good life for herself. She also had to come to the place she realized she was the only one who could get her to that place. She has come to understand everything has not been everyone else's fault, and she has learned to forgive.

We believe the best we could do was to not give up on her. We remained steadfast in prayer, hope, and love for her, and we are so happy to see her growing toward a normal and happy life.

These days we all get along fine, and she has visited us a couple times spending a week with us. She is becoming a great mom and person. She now has full custody of her daughter again and is dreaming of an even better future. Somewhere in the midst of all life's ups and downs, Megan gained a lot of weight taking her to 300 pounds. Instead of being defeated, she realized she didn't want to live like that. She didn't blame life or us for her weight issue, but rather she made a conscious decision to take responsibility for her weight gain and do something about it. She began eating healthier and started going to the gym. Completely on her own, she motivated herself and has lost over 120 pounds. She has become what we called guys like me when I was bodybuilding, a gym rat. She loves it, but even more, she loves the results, and we are all impressed. She just glows and is so beautiful, it is amazing.

With her success in turning life around in such a way, the future looked bright. However, as we have seen over and over again, life just seems to not let her have a victory. She needed surgery to remove all the left-over skin, and they put her on a medication that was an opioid. Her world crashed badly, and the old addiction thing kicked in once again. This time she realized what was happening, and with all the families support, she stopped taking all the medication, suffered through the pain on simple pain killers, and fought her way out of her body's need for the drugs. It was awful to watch, but she did something amazing and got through it. She is again back in a good place after an extreme personal, physical and emotional battle.

Life has not been easy on her, but she has a new found strength and determination. Everyone is so very proud of her.

God made a promise to all of us, and He stood true to that promise for her. Many years ago, He began to work in her life, and He still is today. His promise is found in Philippians 1 verse 6 (NAS), "For I am confident of this very thing, that He who began a good work in you will perfect it until the day of Christ Jesus."

What is being taught here is that when we are far from Christ and salvation, God steps in and begins working in us and on us, so that when the end comes, we will be perfected in relation to Christ and spend eternity with Him. I also think when God steps in and changes us, things like what Megan experienced happen. Anyone who has their life touched by God will see their entire life change as well as their eternal destination. God is good and never stops being good, and the goodness in our lives reflects His goodness toward us. He has certainly been very good to Megan, and what she has received has also brought us all a better, more peaceful life.

Megan is only a couple months from turning forty years old. Connie and I had our thirty-third wedding anniversary a couple months ago. Megan has considered moving to Ohio at the end of this school year. She wants her and her daughter to be part of a large family again. She wants her daughter to enjoy what she took for granted so many years ago. She wants her to have cousins, grandparents, sisters, aunts and uncles, great-grandparents, and especially, to have her mom back in their lives. There is no apprehension or fear in this adventure, only joy. Joy for the move, but also joy for a life that has come so far. Not only that but joy for, maybe just maybe, a family that was dreamed of so long ago.

Notice the difference in her plans. She did not sell everything and buy airline tickets. She called and talked and thought about what would need to be done. She has come to the conclusion that, at least for now, moving would be a wrong move. She realized how much she had in California and how important her father is to her and her daughter. They now just plan a couple visits to Ohio to be around this family. We are super proud of her process in this.

Sarah is in her early forties, has four wonderful children, and a fabulous husband. They are both teachers, and their oldest is now learning to drive. They have a wonderful family and lifestyle and are running the kids all over for sports and school events. They, too, are people of faith in our beloved God and hold Him in the center of their family.

Lizzie is now in her early thirties and is married to a great man. They have three children and have constructed a wonderful life. Lizzie is on staff at her church and home schools her children. Her husband has a great job and is dedicated to caring for his family and works harder than anyone I know. God is also at the center of their lives, and their faith and trust in Him is amazing.

All the goodness we see above is at the hand of a loving God and for that we are so thankful and humbled.

* * * * *

This is a last-minute update. I wrote this book some time ago and it sat. My heart was not encouraged to do what was needed to publish it. I have been working on the publishing part for a while, and while in the process something amazing happened and I chose to insert it here.

It is now mid-2019, and Megan and her daughter have come to spend two weeks with us. The entire family has gotten along better than ever before. It has been a wonderful time, and the past seems to have faded into nothingness.

Megan and I were alone at one point, and as had been the routine, the accusations of my calling her names and abusing her came up again. It was so hard to deal with those comments again. We didn't fight. I just listened, and we went on with our day. I was goofing around in the garage, and in one of those God inspired moments, I was led to apologize. I always defended myself and disagreed with what she said I said and did. I truly believe God helped me to see that it just didn't matter. I had a perspective, and she had a perspective. We would never agree, something had to change. I admitted to myself that maybe I could be wrong. If I was right or wrong, what did it matter? The timing of this was amazing, and just then Megan walked into the garage. I stopped her and told her I was sorry for calling her bad names, I told her I never did anything intentionally to hurt her, but indeed I had and I was sorry for that. I asked her to forgive me. Her eyes teared up, and we hugged. Everything has changed, everything. The entire family has been impacted, and I believe we are forever the family all of us have wanted to be. God has been so good, and in all the mess, we have learned to be patient and loving toward each other. We have learned to forgive and to ask to be forgiven.

I have often dreamt that one day we could share our story in front of groups of families. We could stand there together, unified in the stance that we never gave up, and that with God, nothing is impossible.

CHAPTER 16

Encouraged

The following question is quite similar to the question I posed in the very first sentence of this book. Why have I opened myself up to be judged and criticized while offering my reputation up for bashing? The truth is, I think there may be value in our experience as long and as difficult as it has been.

For the past several years, I kept believing God would not have allowed this in our lives for no reason or purpose. There was fighting, horrible words, meanness, frustration, and brokenness for what amounts to half of my life.

For so many years we dealt with a variety of levels of battling with Megan and her struggles. The battles ranged in intensity, and at times were simply torturous. These past few years it has been difficult to watch as Megan's fought her battles within. It has been a battle we believe she is winning. A battle than may soon be completely over.

She has fought hard these past couple years and has reason to be proud of herself. As I mentioned earlier, Megan did come and stay with us for a few weeks with her daughter. It was a good trip, and we saw the daughter who we had not seen for quite some time and maybe someday will be near us permanently.

For a long time, there has been some Scripture that never left my thoughts. It was and is Scripture that helped me to not give up. It helped me hang in there regardless of how bad it got or how dead I was inside. It is Scripture that gave value to all our troubles and somehow makes sense of it all. Permit me to share the story in Genesis that includes the Scripture that helped me. The entire story of Joseph is found in Genesis 37–50. This is a short version of the story of Joseph, in my words.

Joseph was the youngest of all his brothers and was loved above all his brothers by their father. Joseph had a couple dreams that appeared to elevate him above the rest of his family. Those dreams angered his brothers, and they plotted to kill him. The brothers were off tending the flocks when their father sent Joseph to see how they were doing. For the brothers, this was the perfect time to get rid of Joseph. Although having considered it, they wisely decided not to kill him but sold him as a slave to a caravan traveling to Egypt. They explained his absence by telling their father Joseph had been killed by a wild animal. Once in Egypt, Joseph was bought by one of Pharaoh's officials, named Potiphar, and taken to the palace to serve him. God favored Joseph, and he prospered in all he did for Potiphar. At one point in time, Joseph got into a tough spot with Potiphar's wife who invited Joseph to share her bed. He refused her over and over again which angered her. She told her husband that Joseph had come to her and asked to have physical relations in bed with her. The real story was that she tried to seduce Joseph. He refused, and she screamed to make it look like he attacked her. When she screamed, he ran off leaving his cloak behind, which served as evidence. Even though he had done nothing wrong, Joseph was sent to prison.

While there, he was eventually put in charge of the other prisoners. Later, he correctly interpreted a couple dreams which came true just as he said. Eventually he interpreted a dream for Pharaoh himself which also came true. This led Joseph to become Pharaoh's top man in ruling all of Egypt. During times of great bounty in Egypt, Joseph had a dream about a time of famine which was to come. Because of the vision, Joseph stored incredible amounts of food in preparation for the famine predicted in his vision. When the famine hit, Joseph sold the stores to Egyptians and other countries that came to him for help. Even Joseph's father, brothers, and family were devastated by the famine.

While living in another country, Joseph's father sent the brothers to Egypt to buy food. They went before Joseph to ask for help but didn't recognize him. Joseph eventually revealed who he was, causing great fear among the brothers. Joseph assured them all was well, and he eventually brought his entire family to Egypt where they prospered. It came about that Joseph's father died. Their father's death again put great fear into the brothers. They were afraid Joseph might now get even for selling him to the traders.

Joseph summoned his brothers to him to tell them they were safe. In Genesis 50:20 (NIV), Joseph spoke to them, "You intended to harm me, but

173

God intended it for good to accomplish what is now being done, the saving of many lives".

Genesis 50:20 was always in the back of my mind. I kept thinking that someday all the difficulty we experienced would be used for good by God. All those years of conflict would somehow be given value. For some reason, I could not stop believing those years could not and would not be a waste.

Megan no doubt meant to do damage in some way, least of which would be to make me miserable. There is no doubt she wanted to break us apart and see our marriage destroyed and had said it to our faces. There is no doubt evil was involved in the midst of all that turmoil for I believe the evil one loves to destroy marriages and families most of all. God gave us strength to endure as He did with Joseph and so many others. We held on even though things seemed hopeless. I would like to offer a Bible verse that encourages me.

> "And the Holy Spirit helps us in our distress. For we don't even know what we should pray for, nor how we should pray. But the Holy Spirit prays for us with groanings that cannot be expressed in words. And the Father who knows all hearts knows what the Spirit is saying, for the Spirit pleads for us believers in harmony with God's own will. And we know that God causes everything to work together for the good of those who love God and are called according to His purpose for them." Romans 8:26-28 (The Book)

These verses say so much and reflect what was actually going on in our lives. The Holy Spirit helped us over and over. When I believed our prayers just weren't getting it done, the Holy Spirit must have been praying for us because things were changing and falling into place even though it took years.

What good has come of it? Well, I believe writing this book may be part of that. If because of our struggles, one person or one family can trust that God never abandons us, that is good. If some can see that He has a plan for all of us, even if it takes twenty-seven, twenty-eight, or even thirty-three years, that is good. If one person or family is encouraged enough to not give up and will instead stand strong and commit to keep their family together, then that is the good that will have come from it.

Were all those years of misery worth it to me if it all gives one person hope? If you had asked me that question in the midst of the struggles, I imagine I would have thought that was the dumbest question ever. I surely would have said absolutely not. However, at this point in time, I can easily say yes, they certainly were. We all want our life to matter. Most of us want our life to make a difference. If this is what had to happen to have my life, Connie's life, and Megan's life matter, then it most certainly was worth it. If all that happened to us helps someone see how great God is, then it was used for good. For certainly God is good and no one should ever give up on Him. I know Megan would he heart-fully agree.

I believe what is meant for evil, God can and does use for good. I also believe when you are confronted with attacks and being warred against, God does give you the strength to endure. He may not pull you out of the situation, but He will help you get through it. I kept thinking I was out of strength, but incredibly, somehow, I kept going. I often put it this way, "I was so often at the end of my rope. I was exhausted and knew I would fall. I prayed and watched eagerly for God to take me off the rope and place me on solid ground. Instead, He seemed to keep giving me just a little more rope. Honestly, it made me angry. I screamed at Him, 'I want this all to be done!'" I wanted it to all be over, but He didn't see it that way and gave me more to hang on to. That unbelievable endurance was God giving me strength when I had nothing left and needed it most.

Staying was the right thing and doing the right thing is what I wanted to do deep inside. There were many times I focused on what I wanted for me rather than what I knew was the right thing. Those were the many times I wanted to run away.

I am not able to save lives from a famine, but perhaps my experience can encourage another to pause and think about things in their life or another's life who maybe wrestling with an awful situation.

I have seen and dealt first hand with the damage that happens in a broken home with kids. I am grateful to God my previous marriages never had kids involved because I think it would have been unbearable for me to see them go through what I saw in this marriage.

I feel the need to stop here and say something loud and clear. Not all broken homes and stepfamilies end up like ours. Some work out better than even original families, and some experience even more difficulty than we did. My experience just happened to be one that I believe has been very difficult.

I have also seen the damage it does to families including grandparents, aunts and uncles, kids, stepparents, biological parents, friends, employers, other kids, other parents, church families, finances, reputations, and the list goes on. Broken marriages with kids can take their toll on so many people and things.

In the past couple years, I have facilitated many weddings. I have seen how a parent's decision to divorce has even impacted the weddings of their children many years later. I have facilitated weddings where there is still anger between the parents. I have seen the kids struggle with which parent to invite or if they should have the biological dad or stepdad walk them down the aisle. I have watched kids struggle with whether to invite Mom or Dad, both, or neither. In premarital discussions, I have often seen how the divorce of their parents has impacted their views on marriage and even how these soon-to-be-married couples respond to one another. The trickle-down impact of divorce goes deeper than some couples in trouble may ever consider.

I don't think anyone could predict how many people are caught up in the crisis of divorce. It seems simple enough, the man leaves the woman or vice versa. It appears that the issue affects just those two. How many times have we heard that the kids will adjust? Oh yes, some do but some adjust not necessarily in good ways. If we would stop thinking only about ourselves for a moment, we might see the far-reaching effects of such a decision. I have learned that marital problems are just not about us, they are about many more people than we imagine or consider.

Giving up on our marriages and families makes us liars as well. Oh yes, that was harsh, but I have been divorced twice before, so I feel I can speak on this. I stood there on my wedding day, twice before, reciting my vows that I will endure "for better or worse." Clearly, I lied. Clearly, I didn't mean it. I said it, I may have wanted it to be true, but I did not do what I said I would do. That makes me a liar.

I gave up on two previous marriages with problems that could have been overcome with a little effort. Someone in the marriage has got to take charge and want to make it work. If no one does, it may be doomed.

In stepping in as a stepparent, I have had to deal with so many of the relational interactions of many people. Grandparents wanting the best for their grandkids and protecting them with their whole hearts. Kids hurt by the biological dad not showing up or not knowing how to give them his love and attention, to later realize how extremely important the kids are to him. Moms worrying about their kids and wanting the best for them. Moms trying to fix the kids while they struggle and give their lives away for their kids with little or no thanks. Stepdads trying to do what they can to make a whole family of a broken one. Stepdads never being the "real" dad and always being the bad guy for everything that has gone wrong. Other family members caught in the conversations of angry embattled family members venting and accusing. It is ugly and can drive many people apart forever.

I know the reasons I got divorced the first two times, and those reasons were weak. Now I view the reasons to work it out as much stronger, like simply doing the right thing. We come up with many reasons to split up, we found someone else (well we shouldn't have been looking), not enough sex, (get over yourself, it is not the end of the world), finances (good grief it is just stuff). I have lost everything I ever had for the most part and own little these days. Once it was gone, it ceased to be important. Surprisingly, now I find that I want little, have everything, and need nothing.

At the writing of this book I have no savings or 401k's, nor can I brag about having some grand job in business, but rather that I have not been able to find a job for the past eight years except for a little part-time job for thirteen hours a week. I am very happy. I consider myself a rich man. I've often said I hate my life. I now talk about how much I love my life even though I still have down times. Figure that one out.

Again, I must stop and be clear, there are some valid reasons, even lifesaving reasons, people split up, and it's a good thing they do. What I am addressing is that "some" of us have the lamest reasons to consider giving up, and we should perhaps think about how small and selfish those reasons really are.

This was the one relationship I may have had the most valid reasons to leave, yet it was the one time I didn't quit. I think my wife is better with me here. I think the kids are better, and I think I am a better man for not leaving. The worst parts of my life are the parts I did not run from, and I am kind of proud of myself for doing that this time with God's help.

Sure, I lost much during this time, not all due to the battles but partly so. I didn't get all my needs, dreams, and desires met. I believe I was robbed of many years of a life that could and should have been wonderful. Even now, I still hold some quiet grudge-type feelings, but they are slowly fading, and I hope one day to let them all go. I do sincerely believe if I can get through such a whirlwind of drama as this, there must be many other people out there who can do it as well and do it even better.

I know I am not the "real dad" and even struggle with not being the "real grandpa," so to speak. But I take what I can get. I may be the only one feeling not real, but it is a burden I carry and need to get over. However, I so enjoy being "Grampy" and "Baba."

Walking into that situation I had no idea of what could happen. I was thinking, I will rescue them and all will be wonderful. Maybe not that blatantly, but I thought I could do some good. I meant what I said on our wedding day about marrying them all. I think, thanks be to God, maybe I have shown that.

Please don't unnecessarily give up on your family or stepfamily. Families need great leaders and need someone to guide them through life. The world needs moms and dads who believe in their family and will lay down their lives for them. The world and younger generations need examples of what a family is. We all need people who hold on to God with all they have, no matter what.

Continue to bear all things and give your hearts and love away. Sometimes the most difficult people in our lives grow us the most. Sometimes, as author Dan Millman wrote in the *Peaceful Warrior*, "Those that are the hardest to love are often the ones who need it the most." In my experience, that is so true.

I am no psychologist, but I think most of Megan's anger and behavior came from wanting to be loved deeply by someone and at times anyone. I think she may feel she lost the love she would have received from her father because of the divorce. Later, I think she did not get his love in the way she thought it should be expressed, and it hurt her deeply. I think that when I didn't treat her as she thought I should, she believed I didn't love her either, and I hurt her even more.

Would you agree that the desire to be loved is one of the strongest forces in our lives? We want it even on smaller levels, like in peer groups and from friends. We act, do, wear, and even drive things that will perhaps make us more likable, more accepted, and in turn help us feel loved.

The desire to be loved motivates us all to do amazing and wonderful things as well as crazy, foolish things. Sometimes we want to be loved so much that we actually drive away those we want love from the most.

People have conquered and destroyed countries for love. People have killed for love. People have given their lives in the name of love. Love is a potent emotion that can drive anyone smitten by it in hundreds of directions.

Please look at the big picture. Please consider all that "will" be affected by your decision either way. Please have just one or two more discussions or for that matter ten or twenty more. Don't give up on the power of the love that brought you together in the first place, please. Don't give up on the love and power of God.

Do you remember me earlier telling you I was blessed to have the chance to talk with my first wife some thirty years after we divorced? Meeting her once again, I know that I am not the same person as when we parted ways. However, loving someone and building a life together creates a bond that is never really discarded. If you once loved another person, they may always have a place in your heart. You have each given one another a part of you that can never be taken back.

God spoke to marriage when He declared the two shall become one flesh. When two of anything become one, they cannot be separated without destroying what they have become or were separately. They can never again become what they were before they had become that one flesh. No one can go back and be who they once were for they have changed.

Love for another person is a gift from God meant to last an entire lifetime. These days love and marriage are taken all too lightly. If anyone has any doubt they will be willing to commit a lifetime to that special person, they should not be married. If a couple cannot do "for better or worse," they should not get married.

Marriage, family, and children are far too important to be established on a whim. Such things are also all too important to be tossed aside when things get tough.

Have we worked our way to the family we all dream of? We are getting closer. We are not battling, accusing, fighting, or trying to hurt one another. We are letting God and life bring us closer to the place we hope we can be.

Megan continues to be determined to rebuild her life, and with heroic effort, she is getting close. She has struggled in ways I am not sure I could have endured. It seems her battle with us is over, and her internal battle is nearing completion as well. We are all prayerful and eagerly wait for the day she will have the happy life she truly deserves.

I believe, when she completes this journey, she will be one of the most amazing persons any of us has ever met. Her life has been extremely hard, lonely, and even life-threatening, but she has continued to push on. At the time, she may have thought she meant all those nasty things, but I am confident she loves her mom and family and would never want any harm to come to any of them. Love is the most powerful thing there is and love will win, even if it takes a very long time.

In the Bible there are verses that are often referred to as the love verses. They are found in 1 Corinthians chapter 13 (NIV).

Love is patient, love is kind.
It does not envy.
It does not boast, it is not proud.
It is not rude, it is not self seeking, it is not easily angered.
It keeps no record of wrongs.
Love does not delight in evil, but rejoices with the truth.
It always protects, always trusts, always hopes, always perseveres.
Love never fails.

If we proclaim love, the verses above are the love we should live.

Sometimes we forget how deeply we love and let that love fall by the side of the road on our trip through Angerville and the Town of Shattered Dreams. How do I know? Because I took that trip many times. I took that trip in my shiny, brand new Feelsorryforme pick-up truck. It is a long, lonely trip that eventually leads to Nowhereville.

Give your husband, your wife, your kids one more chance. Once the decision to leave is made, it is extremely difficult to go back, pride will do its best to prevent it. If you do, things will not be the same nor will they turn out to be exactly what you may have imagined them to be because the future has a way of not revealing all it will become.

Give them a chance, give love a chance, give God a chance. It may be hard, it may be full of compromise, it may be full of swallowing that bitter tasting stuff called pride, but the sweet taste of living through it makes a tummy feel good.

God has shown us what love is by sending His Son to die in our place, so that we will not be lost for eternity. God, Himself, made a huge sacrifice to show us He has never given up on us. We mess up, and He forgives us, then we mess up again, and He forgives us again.

If Almighty God can forgive us time after time and never stop loving us, shouldn't we do the same? If we ever want to aspire to something, shouldn't it be to live a God filled life and share a God like love with those we care about?

Sit with those you are struggling with and look deep into their eyes, remembering how strong and powerful your love was in the beginning. Remember how you could not stand to be away from one another.

Remember the day you brought the little one home and how you could not stop staring. Sure, you may be in a time of struggle and trial with him or her, but remember the love and pride you felt? It is still there even if you have to dig deep for it.

When you fell in love with that special someone, you were changed forever. When you discard that person and that love, you once again will never be the same. You cannot go back.

If you are considering marriage, think hard about what marriage is. Having had the opportunity to do so many wedding ceremonies and talk with so many couples, I have learned many couples don't share their views on divorce and have not made a conscious decision that divorce is not an option in their marriage. They give more thought to the caterer, the dress, and tuxedo than they do about the foundational things of their marriage. I have seen the selection of the pastor who facilitates the wedding to most often be the last thing on the wedding checklist. That suggests the physical trimmings of a wedding are more important than the spiritual things.

After talking with so many couples, I have learned I need to talk more about divorce in an effort to help couples be more fully armed as they move forward with their lives. I also hope to help them take a serious look at where they are in their relationship before they get married to make sure they are on the same page.

When God brought Adam and Eve together in the garden, it was a perfect world. There was no thought of Adam and Eve ever splitting up. When God brought them together, it was forever.

Because of the hardness of the hearts of man, divorce was given by Moses. In Old Testament times, the only thing that was unacceptable in a marriage was sexual immorality. Even in that, there was no need for divorce because, in those times, the guilty party was stoned to death. A speedy and permanent solution, indeed, but it shows how unacceptable divorce was. A certificate of divorce was later developed which took stoning out of the equation but opened the door for more misinterpretation of the reason for divorce. Obtaining a divorce certificate became a means to get rid of the old ball and chain for most any reason. It has all gotten way out of control and has gotten even worse in today's world. (There are many good teachings on this that can be found on line. One that is very thorough was written by Pastor David Curtis on Matthew 5:31-32 delivered on October 25, 1998.)

With many people not really aware of the teachings of the Bible, including Christ followers, divorce is quite prevalent in today's society.

That leads me to another thing I address with couples. If they don't agree that God's principles are what they will follow and build their lives and marriage on, then what do they build it on? If not God, then who or what is their authority on what is right or wrong or good or bad? Are the principles of their marriage based on the teachings of Big Bird, a TV psychologist, a talk show host, or mom? What if the couple cannot agree on who they should look to for their principles? I guess then they are each their own authority. That is where I was and where many people are today. We each think we are experts on what is right and wrong, and, therefore, may never agree on how things should be and voila! Divorce continues to grow.

If we have God in the middle of it all, we will have solid, tested, and true principles to follow and agree on, and our marriage has a much better chance to not end in divorce.

God did not intend it to be the way it is and look at the huge mess we have created.

It makes so much more sense to make decisions and agree upon whose definition of marriage we follow before marriage than fight about it years later. Marriage is a serious thing that effects the lives of many people, and it deserves to be taken very seriously for it is meant to last a lifetime.

CHAPTER 17

The Old '55 Ford

After my experience, I especially hurt for the kids. I have learned firsthand they go through so much in break ups, which is not their fault. In a sense they are victims of someone else's choices and decisions. I see them at church, I have seen them in my friends' homes, at weddings, and playgrounds. They are everywhere. Somewhere, somehow don't we need to stop all this? Kids are hurting, families are hurting, all for what? I say again, if you cannot make it through better or worse, don't get married. Some say divorce is too easy, I think getting married is too easy.

Connie was a single mom when I met her, she was giving everything she had to be a good mom to her daughters. Even though she did not approve of Megan's behavior, she never gave up on her nor has she ever stopped loving her. That is something to behold.

Sometimes, it seems guys have a harder time taking such a stand. Some step up and give above and beyond, but I also know of guys that are, for the most part, never heard from again. We men might want to stop and take a page out of the single mom's handbook and not give up. It takes an admirable and great strength to do that. So often, with greatly reduced resources and no help, these amazing women actually perform miracles. Somehow on their own they raise great kids who treasure great memories and for that we all should applaud them.

Perhaps some men really believe the family will be just fine without them. Hold on men! God created the family with the man as the spiritual head of the household. He is to be the guide, the director. He, with the leading of God, is to be steering the direction of the family. Men, you are desperately needed by your wife and children. I lived with the repercussions of a family without the father, and trust me, that role is extremely important.

Kids are precious, they are valued by God, and are gifts from God. How can we act as if they are not something to cherish, protect, and sacrifice for?

Scriptures say God hates divorce. I used to think it was no big deal, but today, I understand how valid God's hate for divorce is more than I ever have because of experiencing what I did.

Words that get said in the battle of a failing family scar us forever. "You're not my real dad" will be with me the rest of my life. Those words are not able to be erased. While it is okay to not be the real dad, the hate and anger behind the words did the damage. Choose your words with care, and what is behind them with even more care.

I also did and said stupid things in the heat of it all, and I offer this advice. Where I realized I was wrong, I did my best to humble myself and apologize to Megan. Sometimes it was used against me, sometimes it was rejected, and sometimes it left the receiver amazed. The anticipated result should not be the motivator, rather it simply being the right thing to do should. Kids need to hear a parent apologize to them when they are wrong. I learned that trust can be built on such a seemingly small act.

I have also described how the kids go back and forth between parents. Sometimes they are manipulative, and I believe, sometimes they are merely looking for a safe place with truth and security. If we are wrestling with issues, the kids will grow in fear of what might come. Never argue in their presence. Go away and fight, but keep them secure. Maybe take a ride in the car. (Smile)

Take the time to check things out. After being caught in a ploy to divide us, we always checked with each other and often found that the stories Megan told one of us about the other were not true or misrepresented. She often tried to pit us against each other. We became wise enough to check with each other before taking any action, offering a criticism, or giving advice. We offered a united front, and a front that we vowed would not be broken. That was a key decision, and one that continued to keep us strong.

Go to your husband or wife and kids right now and give them a hug and a kiss, clear your schedule and go to the park and run through the leaves together. Look at your kids and see yourself, your blood and DNA making them who they are. Look into their eyes and see who they come from, look at some of their behavior and think of the person who helped make them, look even deeper and see the potential they have to become someone awesome.

God created mankind, and you had your part in creating your kids. They are your kids, you are responsible for them, be responsible. If they are step-kids, you made a promise to care for them, do what you said you would do.

Most importantly, bring God into the center of your lives, family, and marriage. My life is a great example of how my marriages didn't work without God, and how the hardest part of my life and third marriage survived with God. Indisputable proof from my point of view is that God makes the difference. I believe, with all my heart, that if God had not been in this marriage, I would have been long gone and perhaps written a book discussing that some things are just not worth the effort. I would have been wrong.

I regret giving up on my two previous marriages, but it really reflected what kind of man I was, and I was not as great a guy as I thought. I also regret using some stupid reasons to justify my behavior and validate giving up.

This time I have no such feelings. I stuck it out no matter how great the cost, and I feel good about that. Not giving up was the right thing to do and exactly what I should have done. I did not do something heroic or amazing. This time, I merely did what I promised to do. On a personal level there was a cost, but instead of regrets that I would carry for years, I am quietly proud that we are still a family. I am happy that no matter how many times I wanted to quit and run, I stayed by the grace of our Lord Jesus Christ.

Regardless of what anyone may think or say about how I dealt with things, I am pleased. Could I have done better? I absolutely could have. I did the best I could with what I knew. I am also humbled because I did not do it alone. God stood beside us day after day. He encouraged me time after time. Whenever I conjured up thoughts of anger and giving up, He replaced them with hope and calm. I know I could not have made it without Him. I know because without Him. I gave up twice before.

Pause, give it all more thought, and give it all another chance, then another, then another. Listen more than you talk. Listen and ask questions, listen and understand. Marriage and families can be saved, they can be rescued. You think the present situation is a mess, it could be much worse. In fact, in my experience, it often is.

I remember an old 1955 Ford I had. It eventually developed problems and started to rust. So, I sold it and got a 1959 Ford. The 1955 would have been fine if I fixed it, but I didn't, I discarded it. I was the self-proclaimed expert and decided it had no value. Today it would be worth much more than the 1959.

Maybe some of us are in a marriage that has gotten rusty and needs some repairs, but as the years go by, we might find what we have, coupled with a little effort, could be priceless. We might also realize we were foolishly being self-proclaimed marriage experts, and the marriage we deemed unfixable could actually turn into something amazing.

Isn't it time we became the kind of men and women we were in awe of when we were kids? Isn't it time some of us become examples of what is good and right? Isn't it time we live to a higher standard?

Scripture teaches that we can do all things through Christ who gives us strength. He gave me strength, and I did it, we did it. I know you can do it, and I trust you will be glad you did.

I wish all the best for you and your families. You have been blessed with a family when so many haven't. Some people live with a burden of sadness about not having the very gift you have been given. You have been chosen to be a part of a family, to love and care for your spouse, and to love, protect, treasure, and teach your children.

Children are blessing that give a gift that can come only from them. There is no greater gift than to have the whole family laughing around the dinner table or to pick up the phone or walk through the door and hear someone yell, "Hi Dad! Hi Mom!"

God Bless you.
I pray the following prayer for all families who may be struggling.

Dear Almighty, Loving, Heavenly Father,
I come to you now in the name of our Lord and Savior Jesus Christ on behalf of any hurting families who might be reading this as well as those who are out in the world and feeling alone and hopeless. I pray for strength and courage for them to continue and to not give up. I pray that they come to you in their time of greatest need and lay bare their broken hearts before you.

Help them to run the full race no matter how long it takes, no matter how difficult the journey. Help them to know, great will be their reward.

Dear Lord, bless their efforts, replenish their energy, replace the love that has been beaten away with a fresh and even deeper love. When they get so weary they find it hard to get up, please carry them. Give them hearts exploding with love, compassion, and understanding. Help them to regain their passion for their spouses such as they had when they first met.

Help these families to be an example of what love can endure.

Bless all who want to make it work, with success. Repair any damage and build new and wonderful memories in their lives that will last forever.

Dear Lord, help them to have a life that amazes even them and to be grateful and thankful to you for what you will do. I pray that such efforts will be rewarded, and that it all will bring you Glory dear Father. Amen, and it shall be so.